Praise for Manis Friedman
and *The Joy of Intimacy*

"A rising superstar . . . eloquent and witty."

—*New York Times Magazine*

"One of the great social philosophers of contemporary America."

—Oxford University

"[Friedman's] popular show . . . promotes ethical thinking in cable markets across the U.S."

—*Rolling Stone*

"A most unusual man who is saying what needs to be said. . . . Provocative and inspiring."

—Bob Grant, New York City
talk radio show host

"Friedman is an energetic and entertaining speaker and writer, exploring with careful wit and compassion the gamut of human behavior. He challenges our notions of such concepts as modesty, loyalty, privacy, and sexuality, and makes a lively and persuasive case for values that may have fallen from fashion."

—*The Hungry Mind*

"Bravo, Rabbi Manis Friedman and Ricardo Adler! This long overdue book is essential reading not only for couples

who want to regain intimacy, but for singles seeking relationship wisdom in a culture of meaningless hook-ups.... Rabbi Friedman addresses the underlying issues that have degraded marital intimacy to the point where sex, even in marriage, is entertainment. He provides the antidote for the ills that plague today's relationships. *The Joy of Intimacy* is written in a lucid and engaging style. It will hold your attention from the first page to the last. I urge you to buy this book! Invest in your relationship, or help a loved one with theirs."

—Miriam Grossman, MD, author
of *Unprotected* and *You're Teaching My Child WHAT?*

Praise for *Doesn't Anyone Blush Anymore?* by Manis Friedman

"Anyone who is either married or thinking of getting married would do well to read [Friedman's] book."
—Bob Dylan

"The message in Manis Friedman's folksy and fascinating book...is simple. It's good to be good."
—*Seventeen Magazine*

The
JOY
of
INTIMACY

The
JOY
of
INTIMACY

....

*A Soulful Guide to Love,
Sexuality & Marriage*

....

Manis Friedman
with Ricardo Adler

IT'S GOOD TO KNOW PUBLISHING
New York

For information, contact:

It's Good to Know Publishing
Brooklyn, New York
E-mail: info@itsgoodtoknowpublishing.com
ItsGoodToKnowPublishing.com

For foreign and translation rights, contact Nigel J. Yorwerth
E-mail: nigel@PublishingCoaches.com

Library of Congress Control Number: 2016905453

ISBN: 978-0-9862770-0-9 (trade paperback)
ISBN: 978-0-9862770-1-6 (e-book)

10 9 8 7 6 5 4 3 2 1

Cover design: Nita Ybarra
Interior design: Alan Barnett
Creative direction and production: Yorwerth Associates

Note to the reader: The stories and examples in this book reflect the issues and questions that have recurred during many years of Rabbi Manis Friedman's public classes and private counseling sessions. However, the characters described and the details of their lives are composites, and resemblance to any particular person or event is purely accidental and unintentional. Names and details have been changed.

The information and insights in this book are solely the opinion of the authors and should not be considered as a form of therapy, advice, direction, diagnosis, and/or treatment of any kind. This information is not a substitute for medical, psychological, or other professional advice, counseling, or care. All matters pertaining to your individual health should be supervised by a physician or appropriate health-care practitioner. Neither the publisher nor the authors assume any responsibility or liability whatsoever on behalf of any purchaser or reader.

To the Students of Bais Chana

CONTENTS

CONTENTS

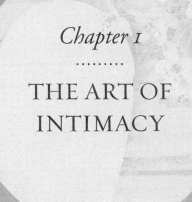

Chapter 1

....

THE ART OF
INTIMACY

The Art of Intimacy

. . . .

INTIMACY IS AN ART. It's not something that just happens. It must be learned, cultivated, and practiced carefully if it is to flourish. For more than four decades, I've been counseling and teaching about marriage and relationships, love and intimacy. What I've found over and over again is a lot of confusion and misunderstanding and, along with it, an equal amount of pain, disappointment, and longing. It seems we've lost the key to fulfilling one of our most basic human needs. Intimacy has become a lost art.

Jack and Alicia's story is all too typical of what I've seen. While coasting through their early thirties, Jack and Alicia had met, dated for the better part of two years, and grown to love one another. Over that time, their relationship had become comfortable and conveniently reliable. They provided company for each other for nights out and weekend engagements. Early on, they had mutually agreed to an exclusion clause in their relationship, one that would protect them from what they called "responsibility creep." According to the terms of this exclusion clause, while they saw themselves as a couple, they nevertheless allowed each other full social independence and freedom. Filled with the vitality of youth, they saw no threat in this set-up.

All such smug sureties shifted after 9/11, a watershed event that redirected the stream of their lives. Dominating the new uncertainties was not only the simple question of physical survival but also a desire for meaning and purpose in their lives. *If I'm wiped out, what will I leave behind?* In the end, the conversation between them came down to this: "If life could end so easily, maybe we'd better get on with the real stuff." Together Jack and Alicia consented to make a marriage, which they came to view as a sort of well of blessing and power at the center of their lives.

The biological imperative that had launched Jack and Alicia into married life almost inevitably led to a cascade of further imperatives. In pursuing and sustaining their personal version of the great American Dream, they were swept up into acquiring the accoutrements of successful American family life: the mortgage on the mini-mansion in the suburbs, the two cars, and the two children (with orthodontia). That was followed by an equally frantic race to avoid foreclosure on that dream.

Increasingly, they had little time and even less energy available to care for their marriage. Worse than that was the damning truth that they just couldn't be bothered. At the heart of their relationship lay apathy. They simply weren't interested in each other or their marriage. There was no intimacy—physical or emotional or soulful.

I have heard stories like this as a rabbi as well as a marriage counselor and speaker. When two married people tell me that they are unhappy or that they can't get along and are constantly fighting ("I'm becoming meaner and more vicious by the minute") or that they are simply bored, I tell them that those are just symptoms. They are not the real problem. The real problem is loneliness. Even though they are together, couples still feel desperately alone.

In talking to individuals and audiences of every age and background on six continents, I've observed that perhaps no topic so poignantly concerns people as that of sexuality and intimacy. Repeatedly, I have been asked: What exactly is intimacy? How does love fit in? Why get married? Can old rules and customs possibly still apply today? When is it okay to give up on a marriage? Does divorce mean the marriage was a mistake? What does Judaism say about sexuality?

Along with such questions have come many sad stories similar to that of Jack and Alicia. This has led me to conclude that the truest statement about marriage today is that it might not last long. There are plenty of pressures that can erode the marriage relationship—financial worries, career-driven insecurities, emotional instabilities, physical infirmities, and so on. Yet of all the issues that prompt people to consider divorce, none looms larger than the loss of intimacy. The skeins of love, sex, respect, and meaning in a relationship have become so thoroughly entangled that couples often have no idea what intimacy really is and what creates it. This confusion is real and it is painful, affecting children and families from all cultures and across all economic classes.

Jack and Alicia eventually realized that shared apathy is no comfort. The growing awareness that neither of them was particularly interested in sex felt like nothing but shared shame and failure. Remembering how passionate they had been when they first met and how exciting it all had been in the beginning, they blamed the marriage itself for the seepage of sexual interest from their relationship.

Esther Perel, author of *Mating in Captivity: Unlocking Erotic Intelligence,* describes the sexlessness of the modern couple as a pervasive if unacknowledged problem. While the numbers are tricky (it's difficult to measure a lack of desire in the married masses), the public response to Perel's book clearly shows that the dilemma is genuine. Indeed, Perel reports that while touring the country to promote her book, she has repeatedly faced "packed auditoriums, vibrant with the energy of the unspoken."[1]

Confusing Sex, Intimacy, and Love

How did we get to this place? At first glance, it seems counterintuitive. In liberating the modern marriage—in making it free from stigmas, hang-ups, and disproportionate allocations of power—we have somehow also managed to free it from passion.

We've been bombarded for the last sixty years with the message that sex is fun, it's healthy, it's harmless—relax and enjoy. So that's what people have been doing. They are enjoying to their heart's content. Yet very few are content. We are probably more sexually frustrated than our grandparents. And while we have seemingly internalized once and for all the teachings of psychology about the importance of expressing emotions, sharing feelings, and revealing what used to be so unhealthily suppressed, many couples are still feeling unhappy. Why, after all this sharing and freedom is there no intimacy?

It is intriguing that this development is not confined to any particular group. It pervades disparate social groupings. Even people who practice abstinence before marriage often run into trouble afterward. While abstinence before marriage may provide focus and help avoid confusion, by itself it does not teach anyone how to behave once married. Without gaining knowledge somewhere, how can we go from inexperience to successful intimacy—whether physical or emotional?

Today's society is unfortunately ill-equipped to provide the answers. To understand and achieve a truly intimate relationship, I believe we must first come to a new understanding of intimacy. Why is a new understanding of intimacy, even a new definition of it, necessary? Modern culture has identified the sexual act as the defining experience of an intimate relationship, so much so that sex itself is called intimacy. If sex is intimacy, why do so many couples feel that even when they have an active physical relationship, they are still missing intimacy? Folded into the confusion is a contemporary understanding of love that is far too fragile to sustain and nurture intimacy.

The language we use to describe our relationships doesn't help either. None of the many phrases for physical relationships that have passed in and out of popularity gets even close to describing what is needed to achieve an intimate relationship. In fact, many of them tend to blur the issue. Consider the phrase "I've been *seeing someone* for the last few months." Really? Where exactly are you seeing her? As she drives by? At the water cooler? One of these days somebody is going to tell me, "I'm seeing a very, very nice woman," and I'm going to say, "Can I *see* her too?" *Seeing someone*—could there be a more superficial way to refer to a sexual relationship?

How about this one: "We've been *getting together* a lot recently." *Getting together* sounds like either lunch at the country club or a grossly descriptive phrase. It does not evoke the idea of intimacy. Another expression is "Jason and I are *dating*." What does that even mean? That we're getting older by the minute?

Hooking up, the phrase of the past decade, conjures up images of mechanical connections. It is perhaps the award-winner for draining all meaning from a physical relationship. The top prize, though, for most successfully making intimacy sound downright boring must go to *sleeping together*. "I heard that Jack and Jill have been *sleeping together.*" Why do they bother? Surely Jill could get better sleep in her own bed. And, of course, there is the expression *making love.* Yet one of the most important discoveries we can make about this topic is that *sex without intimacy does not make love.*

So why all the evasive catchwords? Perhaps they are a way to avoid experiencing the pain we're afraid might come if we remain open and vulnerable in a truly intimate relationship. If a relationship you considered yourself seriously invested in comes to an end, you'll have to say, "The relationship fell apart." Since that experience will be painful, we try to protect ourselves by talking about the relationship in more impersonal terms, such as "Oh, I'm seeing someone." That way if it doesn't work out, we can say, "Okay, so I'm not seeing him." By using that kind of vague language to describe our most intimate relationships, we create a buffer.

It probably wouldn't matter that these phrases don't serve to enlighten us about intimacy were it not

for the fact that intimacy is a serious concern for anyone seeking to lead a meaningful life. Human beings
crave the presence of an intimate relationship because,
for one, its presence adds dignity and meaning to their
lives. Intimacy, however, is more than simply capturing
dignity and meaning. Intimacy is an *essential need*. We
crave intimacy because without it we do not feel whole.

Timeless Wisdom
That Can Save Relationships

Although the story of Jack and Alicia sounds dismal,
it is helpful because it also offers hope. Determined to
save their marriage, they went searching for a healthy
way to handle love, sex, and marriage. Their search
brought them to my office, where, like so many others, they discovered a new understanding of intimacy—
an understanding gleaned from the timeless teachings
of Jewish tradition, including the mystical teachings
known as Kabbalah.

Before we go further, though, I want to clear up something. You may be wondering: *What can a rabbi teach me
about intimacy?* You'd be surprised. The ancient, mystical
traditions of Judaism are both profoundly perceptive as
well as realistic and practical—and they are highly rel-
evant to the intimacy crisis so many are experiencing
today. In addition, you don't have to be Jewish to understand and apply the wisdom and advice you'll be learning

here. Whatever your circumstances, the concepts you'll explore can help you reconnect with your finer nature and restore a sense of sacredness to your own relationship. Anyone who wants to fully give and receive the gift of intimacy can benefit from the insights in this book.

Jewish tradition differs vastly from other religious traditions when it comes to its view on relationships between men and women, marriage, sex, and intimacy. Many traditions hold that if a human being wants to become a holy or godly person, he or she must pull away from earthly concerns, including attachments to other humans, and concentrate on God. Get a cabin in the woods, hole up there, and think holy thoughts only about God. Sit silently on a mountaintop so you can hear the voice of the soul. Remove yourself as much as possible from the activities of human society—don't share meals, drinks, chats, hugs. To some, all the pleasures that derive from human interaction constitute a distraction from the goal of achieving holiness.

The logic of this line of thought is that because this physical world conceals God, it is therefore negative and its demands are undesirable; thus, it's best to get away from the world so that its influence will be at an absolute minimum. In other words, these traditions say that the more you can get away from the physical and the material, the closer you can come to apprehending God.

In contrast, Jewish philosophy, as revealed in the Torah (Hebrew scripture and teachings), expounded in the Talmud (the fundamental book of Jewish law based on the Torah), and explained by Jewish sages, says: "Yes, it is true that the physical world conceals God. So go reveal him from within the physical. How? Use that world in the way God wants you to. Every time you do a good deed, using material and tools of the physical world, you reveal why they were created; and by doing so, you reveal godliness itself. With that purpose in mind, you can go ahead and enjoy this world. You can eat, drink, chat, hug, and get married, but do all those activities in the way God wants them done, and in this way you will reveal his presence in the world."

There is no human interaction so ripe with potential godliness as the intimate relationship between a husband and a wife. On the one hand, this relationship presents itself as an intensely pleasurable physical experience. The lure of this experience has brought couples together throughout the ages, establishing marriages and creating new generations. It has also been exploited throughout the millennia in human society, fueling illicit businesses and prompting immoral liaisons and abusive practices.

Yet it isn't mere physical pleasure that has drawn all those millions of couples together. More than anything else, *the desire to deeply know and to be deeply known* by another is what lies at the heart of intimacy. The intimacy of marriage endures as the most intensely personal communication possible between two people, and it crosses all cultural divides and spans all historical periods.

For many years now, relationship experts have put the emphasis primarily on improving one's physical relationship. Are you getting the most pleasure? Can you be better at it? Now the experts are admitting that they've made a mistake. The mistake is that married couples don't need increased physical pleasure or better physical pleasure. What we need is closeness. Even more than that, we need oneness. We want and need the joy of intimacy.

As you will see, Jewish tradition contains great wisdom about true intimacy—wisdom that has been handed down and cherished for more than five thousand years. This wisdom is as applicable today as it ever was because human beings are the same as they have always been, with an unchanging need for intimacy and a perpetual longing for it. That's exactly what brings so many couples, confused, disappointed, and looking for hope, to my doorstep.

Teaching about this subject is something I am passionate about because the need is so great and because the age-old wisdom I've had the privilege of sharing has helped many couples navigate through their own intimacy crisis. You could say I'm on a mission—a mission to save marriage and help couples create and nurture intimate relationships, one bedroom at a time.

I wrote this book to help you sort through all the misinformation and confusion and discover the sweet prize of intimacy that awaits you. Whether you are young or more mature in years, whether you are single or married, whether you are currently in a relationship or seeking to create one that is both meaningful and fulfilling, *The Joy of Intimacy* can help you learn the art of soulful relationships. Along with the valuable insights that come from Jewish tradition and lessons I've learned through my work over the years, I've included here the stories of men and women who, like Jack and Alicia, have discovered the joy of true intimacy. I hope that in their stories you, too, can find some answers that will lead to the light and warmth these couples have found for themselves.

*The key to sustaining a great relationship
is learning the art of intimacy. True intimacy is
physical, emotional, and soulful—and it
must be cultivated and practiced
if it is to thrive.*

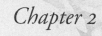

Chapter 2

·········

PARDON ME, IS THAT MY SOUL YOU'RE WEARING?

Pardon Me, Is That My
Soul You're Wearing?

. . . .

MARRIAGE IS AND ALWAYS has been the default means of providing an intimate shelter for the relationship between a man and a woman. While each culture may go about it in its own way, the fact is that people everywhere have been getting married for thousands of years. But why do we marry?

Though the customs may vary, the reasons for marriage transcend culture, sounding a recurrent beat through the ages and across a range of motivations. People have chosen to get married to get away from parents, have babies, achieve financial security, ensure the succession of royalty, maintain a steady sex life, have someone to boss around, have someone to tell them what to do, and have someone to count on at all times. More than anything else, deep down we crave intimacy and we know, if only by instinct, that intimacy demands exclusivity. So we get married.

All conventional reasons for marriage revolve around the creature comforts and pleasures that define the "needs" of our physical lives—needs for safety, financial stability, physical satisfaction, and emotional security. In the past, social custom has dictated that the way to achieve all this was within the confines of marriage. You want to have a baby? You had better get married or the baby will be illegitimate and unable to inherit your wealth. You want food and shelter? You had better marry a man who will provide for you. You want social respect and honor? Marry a woman from a good family, treat her well, and you will be respected in the community.

While these motivations are understandable, they don't feel noble. To many people, they are indications of weakness and neediness and are thus considered demeaning. Seen in such a light, marriage feels not like an opportunity but like a prison. When enough members of a society see things that way, when a tipping point has been reached, the entire society is affected.

We have apparently passed that tipping point. Our culture operates under the notion that we have found ways to get around the old imperatives of marriage. Who needs a spouse to conquer loneliness? Good friends are the best antidotes for that. Financial security? Women can find their own financial security without having to be bossed around by a husband. Who needs marriage for steady sex? Doesn't everybody know marriage kills off the sexual instinct? Ironically, just as we have supposedly conquered the need for marriage, we find that we increasingly suffer from a lack of intimacy.

Intimacy implies a soulful connection with another person, an exclusively private and deep relationship. Everybody wants that. It's a human need. It cannot be picked up on the hoof, without trying, from a casual encounter. A soulful connection implies longevity in a relationship. So even as other motivators for marriage fall away, this one remains as strong and compelling as ever.

Mystical tradition has a take on the story of Adam and Eve that teaches us something essential about our own pursuit of intimacy. The Book of Genesis says this about the creation of the first human: "And God created man in his own image, in the image of God created he him; male and female created he them."[1] According to Jewish tradition, what this means is that God created the first human as an androgynous being, both male and female.

In other words, originally male and female were one being. In Hebrew, the language in which the story of Genesis was written, the word for a human being is *adam*—an *adam* being a whole human being, male and female combined. God then put this whole human being to sleep and separated, physically and spiritually, the male and female parts from each other. Thus they became two halves of one being—one half a man

(Adam) and the other a woman (Eve). Their original combined state, however, had a lingering effect. Because they had originally been one being, it remained part of their nature to seek oneness again. Modern psychology calls it the need for closeness.

Today we're told that the separation between male and female is so vast—that men are from Mars and women are from Venus. But it only looks that way. The truth is that that separation is artificial. To this day, it is still part of the nature of a man and a woman to seek oneness with each other. When the two halves eventually find one another and marry, they make a complete whole again and become an *adam* as at the beginning of creation. Becoming one again is intimacy. The story of Zoe's marriage, divorce, and remarriage illustrates that principle in unexpected ways.

Our Soulful Connections and Separations

It had been seven years since Zoe's divorce from her first husband, Jay, and she felt it was time to try marriage again. She had found a man who wanted to marry her. Although he wasn't dazzling, even in her own estimation, he was no worse than any other possible candidate for the job, and he had some clear advantages over several in the field, most particularly over her first husband.

In Zoe's opinion, the only good thing she had gained from her first marriage was a new surname she preferred over her own. Even now, all these years after their divorce, Zoe could, without much prompting, go on and on about Jay and his attitude toward life. Each recollection of their life together released a new stream of anger, and each new cascade again validated her decision to leave him: "Of course I needed to divorce Jay. Look what he did to me! I deserved a better life!"

Zoe had resigned herself to learning the advantages of being single again, appreciating the independence and tidy quietness of her emotional life. She had remained satisfied until one November evening when she found herself in her parents' home in a Minneapolis suburb, celebrating her birthday in the company of her married siblings and their children. Suddenly, she was hit with the reality that when the party was over they would go home with their families and she would be thirty-three years old and alone.

This time her thoughts carried her beyond her anger at Jay. The shock of contemplating the years of solitude ahead woke her up. Before she fell asleep again, she decided that it was time to find a husband with whom she could share a life.

It took less than six months to find David and another three months for Zoe to be satisfied that though this was plainly not going to be a passionate affair (no swelling music of true love), the two were compatible. His podiatry practice complemented her orthodontic clinic, and they both had a charming set of matching compulsions about punctuality and order. Actually, they were meta-compatible, being at one in the belief that compatibility was a higher order of love. Both were grateful to have found such a meeting of minds, relieved to find social safety, and comforted to discover that neither needed "the earth to move."

So, on these rather pragmatic terms and with clear heads, David and Zoe decided to marry. If there was some natural trepidation on Zoe's part about retrying a task she felt she had so miserably failed at the first time, she buried the self-doubt under plenty of bravado. In the midst of planning for their wedding, however, disaster struck.

Both the happy couple and their parents had agreed that this marriage should begin with a proper ceremony in the synagogue frequented by David's parents. In arranging this, David, who benignly thought he was simply attending to another item on his to-do list, had a preliminary meeting with the rabbi. In this meeting the rabbi made it clear that Zoe had to obtain a real live, kosher Jewish divorce from her first husband—an item the rabbi referred to by its Hebrew name, *get*. Yes, the rabbi acknowledged that David and Zoe were not observant, but he believed it was important to "keep their religious options open." If either one decided to become observant later in life, he or she would find it retroactively crucial that they had heeded the fine print at the time of their marriage. While he commiserated with David about the complication this would introduce into their wedding preparations, he was adamant that Zoe would have to obtain the *get* from her first husband, Jay, or the rabbi would not perform the wedding.

Zoe was incredulous. Her first wedding had been planned in about thirty minutes on a lazy Tuesday afternoon. Jay had remembered that he had a cousin who knew about weddings. They contacted Cousin Gordy, who proved to be a real treasure. He managed to snag what appeared to be a bona fide rabbi to run the show and procured a real wedding canopy, known as a *chuppah,* for a prop. (Jay had thought these accoutrements were cool; Zoe had thought them irrelevant.) The ceremony had taken place in a canyon outside Boulder, Colorado, and had been followed by a picnic lunch. Zoe had worn a purple broom skirt and a white peasant blouse. With difficulty, Jay had been persuaded not to wear his cycling gear. At the time, Zoe had glowed with the thrill of their nonconformity. Now she cringed when comparing that picture to the formal dignity of a ceremony in a synagogue.

"We weren't even Jewish!" she cried to David.

"What do you mean? You're both Jewish, no?"

"Well, yes, but we weren't religious!"

David, fully on board with the rabbi's requirements, intoned somberly, "You still need a *get*. Look, the rabbi explained the whole deal to me. Neither of you had to be the least bit religious for the Jewish part to be real. You had a *chuppah* and since there was a rabbi there, you probably had the other bits needed to make it stick. From the rabbi's point of view, it was a real Jewish wedding and we can't get married until that marriage is over."

"How many times do I have to divorce this guy to get rid of him?" Zoe wailed in frustration. She declared herself in favor of finding another rabbi, but since David had already been persuaded, he nixed that idea as well as her suggestion of eloping to Las Vegas. "What's the big deal?" he asked her. Eventually, that's what everybody wanted to know. What's the big deal? Just find Jay and do the divorce thing.

Zoe wasn't sure why, but putting the why aside she realized it was a Very Big Deal. None of the others could realize the shock she had absorbed in finding out that she was, in actuality, still married to Jay. In seven years, she had not seen or heard of him—not one word—and all that time she had supposedly been married to him! While the others believed that this *get* would simply be a matter of form, a mere confirmation of the secular divorce (which was the part that really mattered), Zoe sensed the truth deep down inside.

The truth was that she believed she really was still married to Jay and bound to him in some way. Bitterness over what had happened in the marriage was to be expected. Zoe was more than bitter, however; she was still as angry as if the arguments with Jay had not ended, as if he was still her current problem. In fact, at this moment, she was pretty sure her missing "husband" was busy doing something that would irk her. What had he been up to all this time?

She turned to Cousin Gordy, the one who had facilitated the first wedding, to help track down her erstwhile husband. After hearing why she needed him, Gordy, ever full of surprising help, also recommended that Zoe get in touch with me, promising her that "from Rabbi Friedman you're gonna get the real deal on marriage."

Two Parts of One Whole

By the time Zoe and I met, she was already dealing with Jay. Although she felt this problem was on the way to being straightened out, this episode had stirred up questions about marriage. And, as Gordy had suggested, she really did want the real deal on marriage.

As I listened, Zoe spent thirty minutes spooling out her tale. She ended her story with the question that had propelled her to this meeting: "Why do I still feel married to this man?"

"What do you mean? You *are* still married to him." As an answer, it lacked profundity.

"No, I'm not. We haven't lived together in seven years. I haven't seen him during all this time. I don't even like him. We got a divorce from the State of Colorado. We split up the stuff. He took our entire collection of

Leonard Cohen CDs—which was not entirely fair, I might add. If that's not divorce, what is?"

I couldn't help but laugh. "It sounds like the opposite of that song from *Fiddler on the Roof*," I said, "the one where Golde tells Tevye all the things she does for him and then says, 'If that's not love, what is?'"

Zoe pounced on this. "Good point. Excellent point. Marriage is doing all those things with a man, happily. And if that's not going on, how could there still be a marriage?"

"So your question is not why are you still married to this man, but why do you still *feel* married to him. You thought you were finished with him and now it seems you really aren't—not only according to the rules, but emotionally, psychologically, and spiritually. Is that what's going on?"

After a pause, Zoe let out a long sigh. "That's pretty much it. I want to add that I don't want to be married to him. I don't like him. He drove me nuts. But when you tell me we're still married, it feels true, even if it doesn't make sense. I ought to feel that I am finished with him, but I'm not. What's going on?"

I think my explanation may have been a bit startling, but it seemed to ring true for Zoe. I said, "You feel married to him because when the two of you got married, God brought together two parts of one soul. You were meant for each other and so God made it happen. It wasn't a mistake. When a marriage doesn't work out and there's a divorce, some people say, 'Well, that was a mistake. We weren't really meant for one another.' But that's not right. It wasn't a mistake. God doesn't make mistakes. It's like saying, 'Oops, I gave birth to the wrong baby. This is not my kid.' You don't give birth to the wrong child and you don't end up marrying the wrong man."

"So how come divorce is allowed?" Zoe asked. She had been following my words intently and was puzzled.

"It's allowed because even though these two people are meant for each other, even though God wants them to remain married, it's too hard for them. It hurts too much and being married is too hard. If that's the case, if we feel we need out, God allows us to get out. He is tolerant of our limitations, so to speak."

Zoe was silent, her mind filling with the realization of her own limitations, how unprepared she had been for marriage, and what a poor sport she had been. Into this flood of self-condemnation, I injected a suggestion. "What you really need to find out about is not divorce," I proposed. "You need to understand what the Torah has to say about marriage."

What the Jewish teachings say is that the unique attraction between men and women originates from a desire to be whole again, to reunite two parts of one *adam*. It is unnatural to be alone, for God originally created the two as one. Their separation is an unnatural imposition, and thus they are told to seek one another and overcome this unnatural state.

Why does God separate us and then ask us to seek oneness again? Perhaps because the search for oneness with another soul is the essential experience of being human. Indeed, that's what makes us human. The other creations, all of the beasts of the woods and fields, do not have this task. They were created spiritually finished, good to go, and ready for their jobs in the world. Not so the human being, the *adam*. The human experience is a quest to unite two halves of one whole.

Yearning for Unity

So why do we desire intimacy? Well, it certainly is not because we want to have sex. The essential and unique attraction between men and women is not sexual but spiritual. What men and women do need and can get nowhere else except from one another is the intimate experience of oneness.

While the unity at the core of intimacy is the main focus of that experience, the separation that precedes it is also crucial. The separation creates the need and the yearning for unity. An example of this is in the classroom when a superlative teacher whets the appetite of the student with information and reasoning and then withholds the conclusion to an argument as he waits for the student to search for and find it. Holding back the answer for a time creates the yearning for it.

Kabbalah, the mystical tradition of Judaism, teaches that this dance is replicated on the cosmic level. God created the world and then "stepped back" from it, separating himself on some level so that we, his creations, will seek through free choice to do good deeds that will unify us with him again.

Becoming one seems almost impossible to pull off but, in fact, a husband and a wife can become one *because they were once one.* The Talmud tells us: "Forty days before the formation of an embryo, a heavenly voice proclaims: 'The daughter of this one is destined to marry that one.'"[2] It then goes on to explain the ramifications of this concept. The souls of a husband and wife are created together and are destined for one another. Therefore, when they marry it is possible to bring them back together. It would be impossible to bind together two souls that were never connected.

Zoe's certainty that she and Jay were still bound together, despite their differences, is testimony to this concept. Seven years of separation could not wipe it away. Another important message from Zoe's story is this: Many of us mess up, but it is possible to gain new knowledge and try again. Eventually, Zoe obtained her *get* and, in the process, she brought to her new marriage a deeper perspective of and commitment to marriage and intimacy.

As I explained to Zoe, in cases where a divorce must take place, a second marriage is also divinely ordained.

No marriage is ever a mistake. God doesn't play dice with the universe. Whenever two people come together in marriage, it signifies a special connection between two souls as well as a distinct opportunity. Getting remarried after a divorce is a renewed opportunity to learn *how* to be married and how to achieve true intimacy—with mercy and compassion, with kindness and consideration. It's a second chance.

What's important here is that our coming together is not just a simple attraction between two people; it's much greater. It's a spiritual connection, an affair of the soul. When a man and a woman encounter one another and know that each is part of a whole, that is the beginning of intimacy. Marriage is about creating a life that embraces and nurtures that intimacy. Intimacy is a state of grace that arrives and then hides. So even if we have achieved intimacy, we must continue to maintain it. We must constantly seek it out, cultivate it, protect it, and nurture it. Anyone who truly wants to achieve an intimate relationship can learn how to do this.

*The reason a husband and a wife
seek to become one is because originally
they were one—two parts of one soul.
Their unique attraction to each other
originates from a desire
to be whole again.*

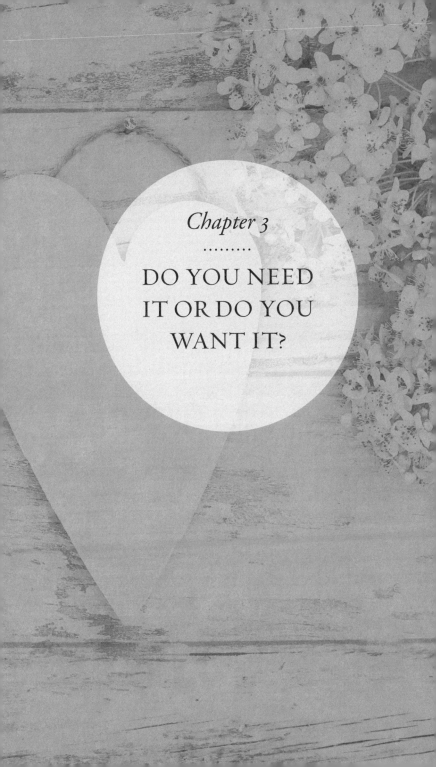

Chapter 3

....

DO YOU NEED IT OR DO YOU WANT IT?

Do You Need It
or Do You Want It?

. . . .

To GAIN A TRUE understanding of intimacy, we must first confront and challenge some widespread misconceptions. Deeply rooted in our cultural landscape are confusions about the nature of sex, what it can or should mean in a relationship, and what role love plays in the mix. Of the many people I've met in my private counseling sessions, Josh stands out as a particularly illustrative example of someone trying to live within the painful constraints of this confusion.

For as long as Josh could remember, he had been thinking about women. When he was about twelve, Josh learned that every other male he knew was thinking about the same thing and, just like him, thinking about it almost all the time. It's an old story, a truth each generation of boys discovers anew and shares in halting moments of embarrassed and guilty revelation.

Over time Josh's pals, like all other groups of boys for generations, had accumulated enough collective comfort with the subject to share their new awareness. Whenever Josh and his friends gathered, it wouldn't take more than a few moments for the conversation— any conversation on any subject, whether it was food, cars, schoolwork, or sports—to veer back to their favorite subject. Within moments, they were making jokes laden with innuendo, comments about one of the girls in school, teasing about prowess and experience. It was during this period that Josh absorbed the important lesson that teenage boys in the back streets of ancient Mesopotamia had no doubt learned: The guy who knows how to get girls wins.

It wasn't as if that sort of lesson needed internalizing. During those early years of the hormonal hurricane, the biological imperatives could hardly be ignored. Just knowing you needed to get a girl was not enough though. You had to learn a baffling set of rules or, more accurately, two parallel sets of rules that governed the behavior between boys and girls. One set belonged to the higher order of one's world, revolving around an idealized theory of courtship that only parents or grandparents claimed to believe in. In fact, no one Josh knew actually lived by those rules.

From experience, Josh had picked up the much more useful second set of rules. As a scientist in this great social experiment, he began to amass solid empirical evidence for what he regarded as the "real" rules. Those included what a young man could and could not say to a young woman, at what time those things could and could not be said, and when to make a graceful exit before getting emotionally stuck. He had become an artist, a master of the art of female persuasion and sexual etiquette. If at age fifteen he was still a bit skinny and gangly, his style was certainly promising.

Every bit of social fortune Josh met with vindicated his methods. Throughout high school and college, he was rewarded (though "plagued" might be a better word) with shocking success and he was the envy of all his cronies. Eventually the thrill of the chase became a drug. His high came from the gratification of seducing yet another girl. Working beneath that gratification was a powerful and largely unexplored premise that persuading a girl to have a physical relationship was proof that she loved you. In other words, each time he ensnared a girl, Josh believed that he was loved.

The Cycle of Unfulfilled Expectations

Common wisdom assured Josh that while a guy could be sexually permissive without risk of emotional involvement, almost every girl wants love to be part of the equation. But Josh was different. Each time he embarked on a new relationship, he sincerely believed himself to be in love. Again. Although his friends thought nothing of two-timing their girlfriends, he refused to do that. For the length of the relationship, no matter how long or breathtakingly short, Josh was devoted. He was a monogamist—an impatient and easily distracted monogamist, but a man who stayed loyal for as long as it lasted. Then would come the inevitable breakup, inevitable because, for Josh, it was almost impossible to resist breaking off a relationship to start over again with someone new. Perhaps the most amazing thing about this cycle is that for some reason Josh never became cynical about it.

With time, however, the cycle began to grow stale. Despite his successes, Josh inexplicably began to feel like a failure. Somewhere along the line, his belief that a physical relationship signaled the presence of love was transformed into a belief that the physical relationship itself *was* love. The physical aspect of his relationships was no longer an expression of love but a replacement for love. He had always expected that sex would bring love and then real intimacy would happen. That expectation was never fulfilled. Instead, Josh began to feel empty, each relationship leaving him sadder and more depleted than the one before. That's not an uncommon scenario for many people today.

When Josh was twenty-eight, he decided to choose one of the women he was dating and propose to her. His marriage to Stephanie lasted about two years and, in reality, was no different from the many live-in relationships he had previously experienced. But when his marriage ended, the fallout was far worse than Josh could have anticipated. He was shattered.

Looking back, he felt that his relationship with Stephanie had cooled long before they had ever reached real intimacy—or maybe he just didn't know what intimacy was supposed to look like. What had begun as a passionate physical relationship, complete with a sense of love, had quickly turned empty. *Is intimacy an illusion?* he wondered.

In analyzing his history, Josh decided that the failure of his relationships hinged on a lack of commitment. While he was always loyal and monogamous in his relationships, he still held on to the ever-present option, silent and tantalizing—even during his marriage—that he could end the current relationship and embark on another. That "opt-out clause" was always there, like a well-devised backup plan, forever holding out the possibility that another woman might be "better" for him, her love for him more complete than the love of the woman he was with now. That is the dilemma of the serial monogamist. He is not really a monogamist at all because there is always another woman present—the one he has not yet met and conquered, the one patiently awaiting his freedom from his current relationship.

Josh also felt guilty about the fact that he had never respected the privacy of his relationships. He remembered with embarrassment how he and his friends shared salacious details of their escapades in the bedroom. He may not have realized it, but besides such behavior being an unconscionable exposure of the women involved, it also precluded any possibility of intimacy. How can there be intimacy if every intimate detail is shared with others?

Five months after handing Stephanie a *get*, Josh washed up in Los Angeles at the home of his friend Adam, who had married Tamar, a childhood friend of theirs. Josh was amazed to discover that these two old friends, who had known each other since before they were ten years old, were enjoying some sort of wedded renaissance. That two people who had known each other for so long could find so much freshness in their marriage was a mystery to him.

Josh discovered that Adam and Tamar had begun observing Jewish laws of marriage, and they were eager to tell him what Judaism had to say about intimacy. At the point they introduced Josh to me, he was ready for a fresh approach. The time for change had arrived.

A Physical Relationship Isn't Intimacy

The term *intimacy* is used freely in society and so the initial hurdle in discussing this topic is to nail down a satisfactory definition of exactly what intimacy is and is not. The common understanding is that intimacy is the same as having a physical relationship, which, as Josh had discovered, does not in and of itself deliver intimacy at all. To bring clarity to my discussion with Josh, I suggested it might be helpful to consider for a moment the analogy of food consumption, which is fraught with similar confusion.

The main reason we human beings eat is to satisfy our need to sustain our bodies. Our stomach demands food because our body needs fuel and nutrients. Once the stomach has been filled, the need for food is gone and we don't need to eat again until the stomach is once again empty. That particular need has been answered and we feel satisfied.

Now consider potato chips. Do we ever have a need for potato chips? For chocolate? Certainly not. We eat those things because they taste good and because eating them is pleasurable. We *enjoy* them, but we don't *need* them. In fact, we eat all sorts of foods that do not contribute to the body's well-being and actually detract from it. These eating habits are dictated by the demands of the palate with little regard for the effect such foods will have on our body as a whole. Some people elevate the pleasure of the palate to a quest, continually searching for the ultimate gourmet experience. Others indulge and overindulge their desire for specific foods that taste good but are not good for them. Although that pursuit of pleasure is legal and may not be harmful to anyone else, it is likely to lead to a heart attack or diabetes if unchecked.

From this you can see that the same activity, eating, can be the means to two radically different ends—to nourish our body or simply satisfy our desires. Is it possible to be confused about why we are eating? Sure it is. Anyone who has ever eaten a bowl of ice cream and then tried to justify it by enumerating the nutritional benefits of the milk and eggs the ice cream contains knows how easy it is to confuse the two.

Since eating habits are comparable to sexual habits, with many of the same dynamics at play, it's instructive to take a closer look at how we eat. When we eat to satisfy our palate, we are not satisfying a need; we are pursuing a pleasure. The essential difference between indulging a pleasure and answering a need is that a pleasure is never satisfied. If it feels good once, there is no reason it won't feel good a second time.

So no matter how many times we indulge in that pleasure, we are never satisfied. There is no such thing as satisfaction when it comes to pleasure, for pleasure only demands more of the same. Even when we pause to take a breather from pleasure, it is merely because we are tired, as the pursuit of pleasure is sometimes exhausting. Ironically, while all of this pleasurable eating is going on, the body's real need for healthy nutrients is not necessarily being satisfied. If, on the other hand, we eat a bowl of nutritious vegetable soup, how much soup do we need? Once we have filled our stomach, we have answered a true need and we are satisfied.

The same options exist in regard to sexual behavior, where the main event is that physical responses are stimulated and the body feels pleasure. The pursuit of sexual pleasure for its own sake will lead a person into all sorts of new experiences that feel good. As pleasurable as those experiences are, however, they do not satisfy any real need. Our indulgence in junk food doesn't satisfy a real need, and neither does our indulgence in "junk sex," so to speak. The demand for sexual pleasure is never satiated. As soon as it is gratified, it demands more. Not just more, but new and different next time. If one had unlimited time and energy, one could keep up the activity unceasingly—that is, until boredom set in.

The Deep Satisfaction of Oneness

What we all have a real need and hunger for is intimacy, which is basic to the emotional and spiritual health of each individual. The satiation of that hunger is achieved in an intimate relationship between two parts of a soul that are seeking to be one again. The only way to satisfy the essential need for intimacy is to put the relationship between a wife and husband into a spiritual context. Since at its point of origin the need is spiritual, so must be the means to address it.

Going back to our analogy, just as eating wholesome food satisfies the physical needs of an empty stomach, so real intimacy brings a deep feeling of satisfaction and completion. But in the case of intimacy, that feeling of satisfaction goes beyond the physical. Of course, the delivery of this very spiritual satisfaction comes wrapped in a very physical activity. The act of spiritual union *is* physically pleasurable. How could it be otherwise? Healthy food usually tastes good; the pleasure that arises from its taste is a bonus. The same is true with the pleasure of intimacy. Nonetheless, the core of the intimate experience does not lie in the physical pleasure but in the pleasure of the intimacy—the oneness it brings.

The bottom line is that the pursuit of pleasure for its own sake leads us to increasingly greater self-absorption without bringing any sense of satisfaction. That was the pit Josh had fallen into, chasing harder and faster after a false goal. As with so many people, this lack of balance at the center of his relationships spread outward, eventually convincing him that something crucial was missing from his entire life. He felt that if he could resolve this core issue, his whole life would look different.

After learning about the keys you'll read in this book and reflecting on the course of his relationships, Josh came to see that he had never really understood what intimacy is and is not. As I explained to him, real intimacy is a far cry from the sheer pursuit of pleasure that leads to self-absorption. Real intimacy, by contrast, points us outward from the self toward another. It lifts us out of ourselves to encounter the infinite in another person. Desiring that kind of intensely meaningful encounter is intrinsic to our true nature, which is why we yearn for it so deeply and feel its absence so keenly.

Indulging in physical pleasure for its own sake doesn't bring true satisfaction. Real intimacy fulfills a deep-seated and fundamental need and nurtures well-being.

Chapter 4

· · · · · · · · ·

PRESERVING
YOUR INBORN
SPONTANEITY

Preserving Your
Inborn Spontaneity

. . . .

IN WHAT WE CALL our postmodern world, many of us typically consider ourselves to be unabashedly sexual beings. We feel we have more understanding of our urges and desires than ever before, and this causes us to assess our options with more confidence than any previous generation. We educate ourselves and our children about our right to do almost anything, almost anywhere, and with almost anyone if we so desire. We have transcended shame and in doing so have seemingly liberated ourselves.

We tell ourselves that because of this we are healthier than ever, free of hang-ups, guilt, and disease. We are grateful for a society where there is no longer any shame in seeking remedies for sexual woes. In our movies, random strangers meet and five minutes later have exciting "romantic" encounters, which we applaud. Of course, we might not do those exciting things ourselves, but we certainly see nothing wrong with someone else doing them. Indeed, it seems almost admirable.

Contemporary society has become habituated to the pervasiveness of sex—to the sexualization of everything. From advertisements, entertainment, and news to social encounters at school and at work, this preoccupation is everywhere. At the same time, the court of public opinion shows a growing intolerance for suggestive innuendos at the wrong moment and with the wrong person.

That is particularly true in the modern work world, where men and women value an atmosphere without sexual subtext in order to do their jobs, whether in the boardroom, classroom, office, or sales meeting. In the business world, a handshake should be only that—a greeting between serious individuals. What might be acceptable, even tantalizing, at a bar (say, a suggestive grin) is seen in the office as an obstruction to professionalism and is considered anathema.

So the handshake, the hug, the peck on the cheek, the myriad other little signs, signals, and comments are, at times, socially innocuous and legally acceptable. On other occasions, the very same acts seem invasive, leaving plenty of room for misunderstanding and insult.

Is It Sex Yet?

The code that governs physical behavior between individuals today is inconsistent and confusing. Which behaviors are sexual behaviors? Which hug is platonic? Which smile is suggestive? In a sense, the question we are asking is this: Where does sex begin?

At the heart of the confusion lie Josh's two parallel sets of rules that young people learn so slowly and so painfully and, it must be said, not without damage. What happens when a young person is aroused by his surroundings or her emotions to a physical response, only to find out that such an arousal is unacceptable or even disdained? Did she send out the wrong cues? Did he misread the signs? Surround young people with the topic of sex, bombard them with it, and then sneer when they misread a relationship as promising more than platonic possibilities. Is that even fair?

In essence, our culture is in the process of desexualizing our young men and women. Desexualization occurs when the natural responses that existed within a person have been removed—scrubbed out and rinsed away. We send our children and they send each other these kinds of conflicting messages all the time. We take teenagers on coed school trips, pack them all into one hallway in a hotel, and tell them: "Now, no funny business!"

Even more illogical, when you think about, is the fact that we take young men and women who are living through the most confusing phase of their lives, put them in desks beside each other for six hours a day, and then tell them: "Get to work! Focus!" As a result, a girl who is desperately attracted to a young man might force herself to tell her pals, "We're just friends," and then find herself having to spend endless time in close proximity to the boy in question. All the while her emotions are being continually aroused and she has to suppress them.

To succeed in such a society means being able to decode some pretty fine print about context. Even for teenagers who successfully master the subtleties—no, make that especially for those teenagers—something precious is lost in the process. In effect, the rules young people have been given are betraying them, killing off some of the inborn sexual spontaneity they were endowed with. That is called "damage." Didn't Freud say something about all of that?

Reading the signs of contemporary culture, the linchpin upon which the acceptability of a particular act hinges seems to be the intention of the act. Whether a look, a handshake, a hug, or a word is sexual or platonic depends on a subjective rule of thumb: What was the intent? Using that measure, a husband might dismiss his weekend tryst with "It was nothing" or "It was just sex."

Intent, of course, belongs to the one who is bestowing the ambiguous gesture. He or she, it doesn't matter which, gets to be the one to determine the context: "I was just being friendly when I hugged you." If it doesn't feel like the giver was "just being friendly," if on reception the gesture seemed to carry suggestive undertones, the fault is said to be with the receiver, who simply doesn't know how to read the signs. In today's rulebook, then, the recipient of the gesture is required to believe the supposed intent and accept the parameters claimed by the giver. If the hug was a bit long, ignited some feeling, or perhaps felt intrusive, too bad. Unfortunately, even if the bestowed gestures are honestly meant to be platonic, they can be destructive because they produce reactions that we must not only ignore but often deny: "Nah, it's cool. We're just friends."

Keeping Our Intimate Instincts Sharp

To put it bluntly, our modern culture is a repressive regime. Its rules dictate a lot of hugging, kissing, and close familiarity with members of the opposite sex to whom we are not married plus any number of ambiguous customs and arrangements that we have to accept, all of which can be stimulating for the normal person. Meanwhile, the rules demand that our normal responses be ignored. It ought to be glaringly obvious that this is a devastating practice. This custom produces people who do not trust their own bodies, their own reactions, and their own instincts. When a person must deny something basic inside and must live with contradictions that don't make sense, he or she becomes fragmented.

Early in my rabbinical career, a group of high-school students approached me with a request. They were heading out on a camping trip into the woods of northern Minnesota for several days. Since they were all Jewish, they had the inspired idea that they might introduce a Jewish aspect into the trip. So they came to me, looking for a way to add some Jewish content to their camping trip.

At first I thought they were joking. "Wait. You're a bunch of boys and girls and you're going off into the wilderness on a camping trip? Together? Doesn't sound very kosher to me!"

They responded with good-natured guffaws. "Ah, no, Rabbi, it's not like that with us," one of the boys explained. We've all been friends for ages. We've known each other forever. You don't need to worry; we could share sleeping bags with the girls and nothing like that is gonna happen."

"If you boys can go on a camping trip with a bunch of girls and share sleeping bags with them and *nothing happens*," I replied, "you don't need help with Jewish content, you need a shrink!"

The truth is that humans are always sexual in the sense that they are supplied with impulses that are always engine-ready. Any encounter is potentially capable of igniting the engine into motion—any touch, any warm look, any glimpse of skin. That sensitivity is not because the engine is faulty. On the contrary, the sensitivity exists because the engine is so exquisite, so finely tuned that it needs only the slightest encouragement to surge ahead. That is the way it is supposed to be. Those are the responses of a healthy person.

However, only the most specific conditions are useful for achieving real intimacy: the right person, the right time, the right conditions. How do we reconcile this? How do we maintain an ever-ready spontaneous nature?

On the one hand, we know that we ought to avoid indulgent practices that destroy intimacy. On the other hand, we must avoid condemning ourselves to unhealthy lives of suppressing natural responses. Stated another way, since arousal is normal, how do we deal with the fact that habitually saying no to arousal is unhealthy *and* living a life of indiscriminate pleasure-seeking is unhealthy too?

The Jewish solution to this dilemma is simple: Cut to an absolute minimum the situations in which we would ever have to say no to arousal.[1] Minimize the chances we might have to become aroused. In this way, the natural energies of physical arousal are relatively untapped, untampered with, and reserved for later, when they will be needed and wanted.

In addition, the Jewish solution says: Do not throw young boys and girls into close proximity, where you will have to engage in the hypocrisy of telling them that they should ignore the normal responses that such close proximity produces. Why arouse them and then tell them to say no to the arousal? *That's* harassment! Taking this advice further, if a woman doesn't hug a man who is not her husband, she will not have to deal with the feelings that a supposed casual hug might give birth to in him. If a man lets it be known that he never allows himself to be behind a locked door with any woman other than his wife, he is sidestepping the uncomfortable stimulation that the awareness of a closed door brings.[2]

The bonus of that strategy is as simple as it is sublime. When it is the right time to be aroused, we can be aroused without inhibition or confusion. Modesty in behavior helps to preserve sexual health, not to suppress it. Its aim is not to suppress arousal but to preclude it until such time as we need it.

While society's casual attitude toward physical contact and sex actually desensitizes us, the guidelines for modesty you've been reading about here protect us not only from harassment but from fragmentation and the dilution of our natural intimate responses. They help us remain whole and ready for marriage, when we will need our natural instincts to be sharp and engine-ready for a healthy intimate life.

*A casual approach to
physical contact destroys rather than
enhances sensitivity. Ultimately, being
modest helps us preserve our
acute sensual responses.*

Chapter 5

....

WHAT'S LOVE GOT TO DO WITH IT?

What's Love
Got to Do with It?

. . . .

OVER AND OVER AGAIN, the message has been drummed into us that if we can just find someone to fall in love with, we will enter into a paradise of intimacy. That is a misconception, and a dangerous one at that. It tries to convince us that love is the essential element needed for true intimacy to blossom. According to this theory, if two people do love one another, they are "through the door" and intimacy beckons. The problem is that when intimacy still doesn't materialize, the legitimacy of any love they thought they had is called into question.

We can hardly be blamed for believing and accepting these ideas, which so deeply pervade Western literature and so thoroughly dominate modern media. We're typically presented with two possible story arcs. In one, two people realize they are in love and initiate a physical

THE JOY OF INTIMACY

relationship. In the other, two people initiate a physical relationship, after which they realize they are in love. Either way, their physical consummation is redeemed or at least made meaningful by the love they have discovered in one another. At the end of the day, these story lines try to convince us that the emotion of love will transform sex into intimacy.

The problem with believing that romantic love is the key to an intimate relationship is that this belief consistently fails those who hold that belief most deeply. It also loads love with responsibilities it doesn't deserve and ought not to have. In this paradigm, love is saddled with lending legitimacy to a union between two people, for without it their relationship is said to lack integrity or even authenticity.

Such a requirement burdens the couple with continual and often excruciating reappraisal: "Do I love him enough? Do I love her the right way? If I am not capable of feeling intense love, will I never achieve intimacy? Will someone ever love me in this unique and necessary way?" Perhaps even worse is the self-damnation of hindsight: "Ah, I thought I loved him, but it turns out that maybe I didn't really love him or I didn't love him enough. Otherwise it would have worked out!"

I see people put themselves through this sort of torture all the time. Even young people, who ought to be full of confidence and belief in their emotional futures, doubt their own capabilities and find that their trust in their emotions is shaken. That is a tragic mistake because, in truth, *love doesn't have anything to do with it.*

Of course, marriages need love, but what kind of love? Heady, passionate turmoil may be intoxicating, but it isn't often useful. In marriage, the kind of love that is useful is a love that has more to do with the right attitude or the right approach to the relationship rather than the kind of love that is concentrated on "feelings." Intimacy flourishes in an atmosphere that is permeated with kindness, respect, and sanctity. True love grows within that atmosphere as well. On the day Debby stumbled into one of my classes, we were exploring that very subject.

More Important Than Emotions

On that particular rainy Sunday, Debby had arrived at a Jewish Community Center (JCC) in Chicago to find that the class she had planned to attend had been canceled. When Amy, the director of youth services, suggested that she might want to check out what was going on in the library, Debby was game—she had nothing better to do.

At the door to the library, Debby was surprised to hear laughter coming from inside. "What's going on in there?" she asked Amy. Searching among the pile of papers she was holding, Amy pulled out a brochure and said, "Here's the flyer." According to the brochure, the talk was entitled "What's Love Got to Do with It?" and the subject matter was marriage, love, and sex.

Debby glanced into the library, saw a white-bearded rabbi at the front of the room, and whispered to Amy, "*That* guy is talking about *sex*?"

Amy nodded knowingly. "Yeah, don't you know? The Chassidics have the inside dope on this topic. Go in and check it out."

We were deep into a discussion about love and its place in a relationship. As Debby joined us and got caught up in the stream of ideas being shared in the room, she couldn't decide what was more shocking— the teachings or the teacher. She had never heard of a class like this, and she could have used one long ago.

After the class was over, she hung around and she and I had a long and thoughtful discussion. Like many, Debby was the child of divorced parents. The divorce took place when Debby was eleven years old. It had been acrimonious, the arrangements for her care strained, and the result unhappy, particularly the estrangement from her father. Since the divorce, she and her mother had shared a life together, reduced not only in means but, more significantly, in morale. The house they had moved into (where Debby, now thirty, was still living with her mother) was adequate and met the standards of working-class comfort, but it bore no resemblance to the mini-mansion that housed her father's second family. Her mother, and Debby by association, dwelt in resentful alienation, angry at the reduced circumstances of fortune, family, hope, and happiness.

Debby's sorrow over these limitations opened her to the sorrows of others, which she instantly absorbed. Her sincere sensitivity marked her as the irresistible confidante of many a sad soul. By the time she was an adolescent, she'd had a natural empathy for others and developed it into a sharply honed talent for discovering, lifting up, and carrying another person's pain. Indisputably valuable to those she helped, Debby was only dimly aware of how needy she herself was.

Her craving to be needed did not make her any less sincere, but it certainly increased her vulnerability to mistreatment. The first injury came from a girlfriend, who used her and dumped her. That was only the beginning. Most of the abuse that followed came from boys and later men she had relationships with. She was careful not to blame these "friends," not only out of a spirit of forgiveness but because she was not prepared to admit to herself her own responsibility in enabling these unhealthy relationships.

That understanding did eventually dawn on her. Debby realized that although each of the men had needed her, their need was not as great as her need to be the "sustainer." The emotion she had felt toward them was warm, sympathetic, and inclusive, and she had called it love. Beyond that, she hadn't really shared much with any of these men. Their joint lives in the months or years they were together had centered on the continual reevaluation of how potent their love for each other might still be. The essential question and the sole qualification for continuing the relationship had always seemed to be "Is the connection still strong?" The validity of the relationship turned on the emotion of love, and when it weakened, as inevitably it did, she felt there was no life to be shared any longer.

It was clear to me that the type of love Debby was describing had not led anywhere but back toward the participants themselves. It hadn't helped them move onward together. Instead, it had only caused them to look at each other and wonder "Do we still have it?" That was the point where being "lost in love" actually felt like being lost. Because love was everything, it was the only thing; and obviously that wasn't enough to sustain a long-term healthy and intimate relationship.

When I said this to Debby, she protested: "Surely love matters!"

Of course love matters. There needs to be love within a relationship, certainly in a marriage. The question is, what is its proper place? In any relationship the most important thing is the foundation, the truth, of the relationship, not the feeling. Feelings rise and ebb. A strong foundation, however, is stable and unchanging.

Like other emotions, love is rooted in and belongs to the soul of the person it arises from. Emotions are a response to influences from both within and without. Those emotions remain the private property of the individual who feels them. While love, one of the strongest emotions, may be stimulated by another person, it does not necessitate the participation of that person. Love can remain private and unshared and still exist. Because of this a man, for example, can love a woman without her knowing she is loved and without his love being reciprocated. Even in a case where someone loves the "wrong" person from a distance, in which case the love is inappropriate (such as loving someone else's husband or wife), the love still belongs to the person who feels it. Of course, you can feel love and not act on that feeling. Lots of poetry and songs have described that scenario.

Unlike love, intimacy cannot exist without the participation of another. While love is about "me," intimacy is about "us." Intimacy occurs when two people become one. For this to happen, all resistance between the two must be removed; they must both surrender completely to the intimate act. Removing all distractions and extraneous elements that might try to come between them enables intimacy to take place. When the time and place is right, a husband and wife open themselves up to the joy of real intimacy. Most of the guidelines in Judaism concerning marital life center around the removal of these extraneous elements,[1] which you'll read more about in coming chapters.

Respecting Your Spouse's Individuality

Intimacy is *inter*personal, and in interpersonal interactions there are rules of engagement. Just as there are rules that assist and enhance the intimate union of a couple, there are rules that demand respect for the personal boundaries of each partner. It may seem paradoxical that, on the one hand, union is what we're after and, on the other hand, respect for the separateness of the individuals involved is the way to achieve it. But that's the reality. In fact, not only must a husband and a wife respect each other's individuality, but they must revere it in order for intimacy to take place.

Let me explain. A woman who respects and protects the integrity of her husband must view him as a separate person, complete with soul, emotions, and thoughts that contain more than she will ever know. When she is allowed to enter into his most private and confidential space, she cannot but be aware of the privilege this implies. Being granted privileges humbles a person and makes her grateful for the privilege granted. Likewise, a husband who is allowed to enter the sacred space of his wife's most personal self must understand this to be a privilege and should approach that privilege with a feeling of reverence as well. When these two allow each other, if only temporarily, into the most intimate part of their lives, they have a shared experience that is intimacy. That shared space is not only intimacy; it is sacred.

Love doesn't actually have much to do with creating this sacred space. On its own, love simply doesn't have what it takes to make this miracle happen. Love will not demand that one revere the other's separateness. As a matter of fact, it is more likely that love will want to consume the other whole, as in "I love you so much, I want all of you."

Once again, true intimacy respects that "all of you" belongs to you; and if you invite me in, it's a privilege. It's not "I love you; let's be intimate so I can have all of you." Instead, it's "You have allowed me to be intimate with you, and now that we are intimate, I love you." Within this paradigm, *love is the result of intimacy, not the cause of it.*

When a man looks at a woman and wants to draw closer to her, he sees that she is a whole person with a richly variegated life revolving around issues and beliefs that he doesn't yet understand. In other words, she has a life already fully formed. He wants to be part of that life, close to what is important to her. Actually, he wants to matter to her as much as her core issues. That is healthy.

What happens if what is at the core of a woman's life is *only* her love for him? If her life is dominated or defined by her passionate love of him—as the language of romantic literature likes to put it, suggesting that therein rests the "exaltedness" of romantic love— there is little chance for intimacy. In such a case, little is being shared because there is little to share. In reality, all-consuming love, the great brass ring of classical romance, is not intimacy. Instead, it is neediness and it obscures rather than facilitates intimacy. Intimacy happens when the woman has a life and the man has a life and they want to share their lives. By sharing, they become intimate, and being intimate brings love between them.

Putting Love in Perspective

Another trap to be aware of, one that is also centered around a fixation on "me," is the subtle idea that "my love for you is what makes you most important—and if I stop loving you, you will become worthless." It's so arrogant to think that our love for another person is what makes them important. Our love does not confer importance upon another, nor is it by itself all-important. Rather, love is appropriate in a relationship *with those who are important.*

That is a subtle but important distinction. Have you ever heard a mother say to her children: "If you don't love me, that's okay because, you know, you're not the only children in the world. The neighbor's children love me—and they are cuter than you." No mother would ever say that because a mother does not need love from her children; she needs *her children's* love. You want your child's love because it's your child. You're not looking for love in the generic sense; you want *their* love.

Likewise, in marriage you are mature enough that you want *your spouse's* love. Why? Not because you have been underloved and are needy but because it's him or her. You want *their* love because they are important to you.

Intimacy is a connection between two people that transcends all "things." There are relationships that are created around things—for instance, you both like piña coladas and walks in the rain. But is that grounds for marriage? You both like to play tennis. Is that grounds for marriage? You both want love. Is even *that* grounds for marriage? Think about it: if you're interested in getting love when you enter into a relationship, who are you marrying? The person or the love?

Love is a very lovely thing, but it's not the person. If you look through the Torah, God doesn't say to his people, "I love you." He says, "Be mine and I will be yours." That tells us that a real relationship is about your spouse, not "something about" your spouse. "*You* have to be in my life, not something I get from you."

If wanting "love" by itself is the theme of a marriage, the whole marriage is endangered. You now have a big condition to the marriage: "Love me or else. Watch your step, because I can replace you." That's not a marriage; that's a negotiation or a terrible threat. If a husband feels that way about his wife (or vice versa), she was never a her; she was only a thing.

Again, this comes around to the truth that when you get married, you're not looking for pleasure or even for love. You're looking for that unique closeness, that intimacy with your husband or wife. If, instead, your need for getting married is to get love (or sexual pleasure, as we looked at in chapter 3), when do you ever have enough? When are you ever going to be satisfied? Marriage means you are never alone, and in a healthy marriage your need for intimacy really does get satisfied.

You can see, then, that intimacy is much more significant and powerful in a relationship than love. It is holier than love. In order to give intimacy a place where it can exist, a couple must create a shared life together. That is marriage. We cannot control or predict what kind of love may come or how long it will stay, but we can create conditions within marriage where intimacy can flourish. Those conditions, constituting the very structure of the marriage, produce intimacy. From that comes the stability needed for love to take root and grow. That's how we arrive at true love. First, there must be respect for the integrity of our spouse, kindness and courtesy in the way we treat each other, and reverence for the sanctity of the intimacy between us. Then from this, true love emerges.

True love is not the heat of passion. *True* love means that we love the truth, the reality, of our relationship with our husband or wife. In truth, if kindness is there, if generosity is there, if reverence is there, what's not to love?

*More important in a marriage
than passionate feelings of love are
respect, kindness, and generosity.
Those conditions must exist for shared
intimacy to flourish, and only
then can true love follow.*

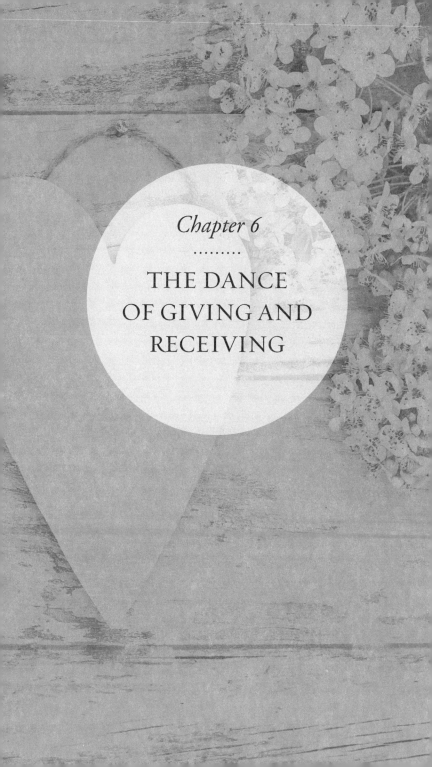

Chapter 6

....

THE DANCE
OF GIVING AND
RECEIVING

The Dance of
Giving and Receiving

. . . .

Two weeks after Debby attended her first class at the JCC, I received a phone call from her. Some of what we had spoken about had gotten her so riled up that after stewing about it, she had finally gone to the trouble of tracking down my number.

"Look, your whole speech over there about love not being the main thing in a relationship was very interesting and everything, but there were some really important issues you left out."

Receiving such impassioned calls is not an unusual occurrence for me, and so I asked warily, "What did I forget?"

"Well, I don't know if you forgot or maybe you just don't have an answer. Because there isn't any answer to this problem as far as I can see."

Debby's problem, it turned out, was a concern that she claimed was shared by women all over the globe. In the world of "sexual economics," women were the "providers of sex" and men were the "purchasers," or to put it slightly more delicately, men were the ones who were trying to gain access to what women could provide. That equation laid a disproportionate burden on women in deciding the parameters of an intimate relationship. To Debby, there seemed no getting around this. In being pressed for sex, a woman usually heard from a man that he loved her. Handling this kind of situation seemed daunting. How was she to respond?

The truth is that Debby was right. That is the way God created men and women. Women are the ones who grant access to intimacy—physical, emotional, and spiritual—while men are the ones who pursue women, seeking permission for that intimacy to occur.

The Interplay of Masculine and Feminine Forces

The differences between man and woman are by design, and those differences aren't only physical. Everything in the physical world is also mirrored in the spiritual world or, more accurately, every spiritual concept or attribute is embodied in some way in a physical object. The fact that men and women are physically different is mirrored in the spiritual realms, where there are forces that we recognize as being masculine in nature and those we deem feminine.

Those forces were created by God as fuel by which good deeds might be achieved. By their nature, the masculine and feminine forces seek expression through action. Their ultimate aim is to bring more godliness to the world, but they seek that end in different ways. They are, in short, the two main paths to connecting with the divine.

One of these paths is characterized by pursuit and action. On this path, a person seeks to remove all opposition to holiness. The aim is to get out there, find evil, and do away with it. The starting point of this path is the premise that, as things stand, there are flaws and imperfections in the world and there are needs that must be filled or injustices that must be corrected. An integral part of this impulse toward action is that it seeks order, wants to create an understanding of God, and labors intensively toward that end. That is the masculine path to God.

On the other path to connecting with the divine, an individual apprehends that the world as God created it exudes inherent holiness, and the individual seeks to nurture and protect it. It is as if the person on this path says, "There is much that is already divine by its nature. I need to take it in, protect it, and help it flourish." This person recognizes that there are aspects of God that are far beyond anyone's hope of understanding, that there is much about God that needs to be accepted rather than understood, and that we can gain a great deal by doing so. That nurturing and receptivity is the feminine path to connecting with God.

Every man and woman operates by a combination of these instincts, and there are times and situations that demand more of the masculine or of the feminine approach. In fact, during whole periods in the history of various cultures and peoples, the exigencies of the time demanded the predominance of one or the other of these two spiritual paths. In general, women have more often followed the feminine path and men the masculine.

The differences between feminine and masculine are at the root of what the Zohar, the foundational book of Kabbalah, calls "the dance of life." In this dance, giving and receiving are the basic forces underlying the rhythm of movement between humans and God and between women and men. Both giving and receiving are essential. If everyone were giving, it would create conflict and chaos, with much energy unleashed but not going anywhere. Energy needs to go somewhere—it needs to be received. Alternatively, if everyone were receiving, there would be emptiness and hunger with no relief in sight. In short, the dance of life requires both giving and receiving.

Without Vulnerability, There Is No Intimacy

The dance of giving and receiving is of particular importance when a husband and wife are intimate. In the physical act of sexual intercourse, a woman receives her husband. That is significant when we remember that their physical bodies were created to reflect a spiritual reality. A woman may be more active in other areas of her life or a man more passive, but in the bedroom it is no mistake that the man gives and the woman receives.

At the ultimate moment of intimacy, when a man experiences the total masculine pleasure of giving and a woman experiences the total feminine pleasure of receiving, they are mirroring the energy that passes between God and his creation. On the cosmic level, God is a giver, the originator of life and blessing, and we, his creations, are the recipients of all this goodness. Understood in this way, the relationship between God and his creation is the dance of life—intimacy writ large.

Although it is natural for a woman to want to provide a welcoming space—to receive—in order to be able to do so, she must feel secure. Security allows her to open up and surrender herself to the task of nurturing. If she were to feel threatened or in danger, she would close herself up and cut herself off from her ability and desire to nurture and to cultivate.

When a woman does feel safe and secure, not only can she nurture others but she positively hungers for something to nurture. That hunger is qualitatively different than a man's desire to conquer. A man who conquers, even when he is conquering injustice or evil, is acting out of an aggressive impulse. His actions are projected outward, away from himself. Not so the woman who hungers to receive and nurture life, who welcomes the opportunity to care for others and beckons others into her circle.

When God rebuked Eve after she and Adam ate from the Tree of Knowledge of Good and Evil, God told her, "You will hunger for your husband."[1] She hungers to receive because receiving is nurturing, and her hunger is impossible for a healthy man to ignore. Indeed, the Jewish sages say that what at first appeared to be a curse has turned into a blessing; for when men discover how much women yearn for a husband, they become receptive to marriage and seek a wife. True giving is always in response to a hunger.

A parallel experience to this type of hunger is the example of a student who is hungry for knowledge. The student's desire to understand stimulates the teacher to explain. The student's hunger for knowledge is, for a conscientious teacher, stimulating and impossible to ignore.

The need to receive and to give is all part of the dance of life that begins with Eve. Her need to receive and nurture initiates all the action. That is why she is named Eve—*Chavah* in Hebrew, which means "the mother of all living things."[2] Ultimately, her need to harbor and nourish life drives the dance that will make a man out of a man.

At the moment of intimacy, each of the participants needs the other acutely. Mutual need and vulnerability are at the core of intimacy—in fact, they define it. The giver needs to be received; the receiver needs the gift. Any time we devote ourselves to giving—any type of giving—and are rejected, the devastation we experience is awful. It feels like a rejection of our entire being. As awful as this rejection is, it pales beside the catastrophe that ensues if a receiver is mistreated. When out of complete trust we have abandoned all defensive measures and have surrendered ourselves totally to the giver, our vulnerability is such that, if we are treated insincerely or unkindly, we are wounded to the core. Because of this, most Jewish laws protect the receiver, the woman, who is more vulnerable than the giver, the man, in the marriage relationship.

So Debby's point was beyond debate. Women do find themselves in a vulnerable position in a world ruled by what she called "sexual economics" and what Kabbalah calls "the dance of life." But then so do men. When real intimacy exists between a husband and a wife, they are both exposed and vulnerable. Without this vulnerability, there can be no intimacy. Engaging in real intimacy is risky, but the respect and protection of the vulnerability that gives birth to intimacy make it infinitely precious.

*Giving and receiving are
the two partners in the dance of life.
By respecting and protecting these forces
and surrendering to them, we achieve
the joy of true intimacy.*

Chapter 7

....

THE CALL OF
THE WOMB

The Call of the Womb

. . . .

No matter how much two people prepare for sexual intercourse, no matter how much foresight and foreplay are involved, the exercise will not go far if they are not attracted to each other. It's common to encounter the question of attraction at couples' retreats. People tell me how they had been so attracted to each other at the start of their relationship. Then somewhere along the line, one or both of them lost that passion for the other. Is it just the wrinkles, the gray hair, the extra pounds? If so, then we are sunk, because we are all going to get wrinkles and gray hair and, if not extra pounds, then certainly sagging skin.

So which part of sexual attraction is in the mind and which part is in the flesh? Here's a story that gives some insight into the dynamics at play.

An elderly gentleman had been widowed for many years and lived alone without any problems. Suddenly he fell ill and his kindhearted, widowed neighbor got word of his illness through the reliable neighborhood grapevine. She prepared chicken soup and other delicacies and delivered them to his door. While in his apartment, she puttered around doing dishes, tidying up, and seeing what else she could do to be of assistance. After about three days of this treatment, the man placed a frantic phone call to his son.

"Son, it's an emergency. You've got to come right away."

The son was alarmed. "What's up, Dad?"

"It's my neighbor. She's in my house all the time. She's bringing food; she's cleaning up. It's terrible."

It took a while for the son to understand that the emergency his father had called him about was what might happen during the private moments while his father and his neighbor were alone together in the apartment.

"Dad, you gotta be kidding!" the son said. Mrs. Simmons is 84! You're 75! And you're sick in bed!"

"Son," the father replied, I can see that you still have a lot to learn. Don't you know that the *yetzer hara,* the evil inclination, can make me well and her young?"

Now, that is a healthy sexual appetite. It is also a healthy appreciation of the sexual attraction between a man and a woman. She is a woman, he is a man—why couldn't something happen?

Of course, physical attraction itself does bring people together. Youth is attractive, especially to other youth, and adolescents discover early on how to make themselves feel good. But they may not realize how such early sexual experiences will affect them. Lots of shallow sex and the fixations that dominate it—chief among them the prioritizing of physical beauty above other qualities—can become obstacles to intimate relationships. Sometimes it appears as if our society as a whole is stuck at an adolescent level of appreciation of what happens when two people have a physical relationship. That's a problem, because real intimacy is for adults.

In one of our conversations, Debby articulated a concern that reflects our society's fixation on physical attractiveness. Until she began to learn more about Judaism, when she was still a fairly young thirty-year-old, she had abhorred the idea of getting pregnant—despite the fact that she behaved like a mother to most people she met. Like many women, she was afraid that when she became pregnant, she would become less attractive and less desirable and that once she had a baby she would have moved from the category of young and interesting to the category of mature and dull.

That reflects a tragic misconception of the power of the womb, a misconception about its attractiveness. For in reality, there is no power in the whole dance of life like the power of the womb. It initiates and moves all the participants in the dance.

The Ultimate Place of Compassion

Both the Hebrew tradition and language can help us better understand the role and power of the womb. In the first chapter of the Torah, we read about the creation of the world, an act God accomplished by speech: "And God said, let there be..." He spoke and everything came to be. The language in which all this was done was Hebrew and so we call Hebrew the "Holy Tongue," it being the language of creation. The Hebrew name for every created object thus becomes not only a name that identifies the object, but *the* name, powerful enough to instruct us about the purpose and essence of that object.

In Hebrew, the word for the womb is *rechem,* a word etymologically related to the word for compassion, *rachamim.* The womb is the ultimate place of compassion because there the mother and father make possible a new life, which is the ultimate act of compassion.

Significantly, there is no other word in the Torah for a woman's reproductive organs, which are called together by this one name, *rechem.* The reason the external organs are not given separate names is because independently they don't have importance; they are considered simply parts of the womb. The core of a woman, the source of her magnetic energy and her attractiveness, is her womb. Within the dance of intimacy, it is the womb that beckons the husband and the womb that receives him.

That is highly instructive. Sexual practice in the

contemporary world is distracted by the external sexual organs of a woman and makes their stimulation and satisfaction one of the priorities in the experience. While it goes without saying that a woman should enjoy sex and that her husband should make sure he is doing all he can to make that possible, being preoccupied with the external organs shortchanges a woman's deepest need—the need that emanates from the womb itself.

It also shortchanges the experience of the husband, as the depth of his experience lies in the heady realization that his wife gives herself entirely to him. In this context, giving herself to him entirely means giving access not only to her body but to her inner self, which involves the hunger of her womb. That kind of submission arouses him, stimulating his deepest need—the need for her. An exercise where the mere stimulation of external organs plays the central role pales in comparison to this kind of satisfaction.

Our Need to Be Known

In the Torah, the intimate act is referred to as "knowing," as in "Adam knew Eve."[1] As human beings, every one of us feels that our significance in this world rests on being understood, on being "known." We crave it. Indeed, it is so important to us that if we feel that no one knows us, we suffer real angst. A sexual encounter is about as personal as any encounter can be, and if we have participated in it but not been known, it hurts. Stimulating and satisfying the external organs is something anyone can do to anyone else. But it is not "knowing" the other person intimately, nor is it experiencing the deepest truth of intimacy

That truth is that at the moment of intimacy, at the moment of oneness, husband and wife are not *sharing* something; they are not giving something they possess. They are dissolving into each other. They are giving and receiving *themselves.* And there is nothing you can get from your spouse that is more meaningful than your spouse.

At the moment of oneness, a husband must respect and acknowledge that at the core of his wife is a hunger to receive into herself, while the wife must respect and acknowledge that the power of her husband is to give himself. That knowledge brings deep satisfaction.

The core of a wife's sexual self finds expression in her womb, and quite obviously what the womb wants is to receive her husband. That is true even when a couple has no plans to have a child or when there is no possibility of having a child, as when the wife is already pregnant, is unable to conceive a child, or is beyond the years of child-bearing. Even if the womb has been removed, the truth of the womb dictates the dance, and it will do so regardless of whether or not we are cognizant of that truth. A husband and a wife who behave in accordance with this deep truth are able to tap into the essence of the true intimate experience. That is, in fact, why we call it intimacy and not sex.

❦

"Knowing" another person
means being attuned to the deepest truth
of that person. True intimacy is called
"knowledge" because it comes from giving
our partner complete access
to our inner self.

❦

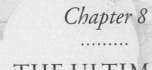

Chapter 8

·········

THE ULTIMATE
PLEASURE

The Ultimate Pleasure

. . . .

PLEASURE IS AN ESSENTIAL part of intimacy. Yet we are often confused and even conflicted about it. That's not surprising. The experience of pleasure lies deep within the web of our human functions, and our attitudes toward pleasure are tangled up in a mix of family attitudes, customs, and practices.

Certainly that was true in Zoe's case. You read in chapter 2 that Zoe and David's collision with the need to obtain a *get* had forced them early on to confront some basic issues about marriage. Initially, they decided they would adopt what Zoe called "the big ideas" of Jewish marriage. They soon learned that big ideas often turn on small details. Zoe and David began to get bogged down. The sticking point seemed to be their idea that the Torah would interfere with the way they wanted to pursue their pleasures. Zoe told me that she considered it "meddlesome and impertinent for rabbis to try to dictate what a husband and wife do behind closed doors."

"*Dictate?*" I exclaimed. "Try *beg*. Try *implore*."

As I explained my views to Zoe, she was surprised that a rabbi like me would acknowledge at all that there is pleasure in the sexual act. It wasn't that she thought I didn't know about that; it was that she had the sense, somewhere deep inside, that this pleasure was in some way stolen, enjoyable only because it was sinful, and therefore I wouldn't approve. Where had that idea come from? For that, we must go back to the upbringing of Zoe's mother, Betty.

Betty's parents were Holocaust survivors. They were somewhat observant, obsessively hardworking, and generally buttoned up about Judaism. Like many children of survivors, Betty's upbringing was laden with tacit guilt at not being enough or doing enough to compensate for her parents' losses. Of course, her parents hadn't intended to burden Betty with guilt; it happened as a result of who they were and what they had survived.

As she came of age, Betty did not work out her confusions on a psychoanalyst's couch, she did not write an angst-ridden American novel about coming of age in the Age of Cynicism, and she did not become a political activist. Instead, she went to Brooklyn College, where she got straight As, became a nurse, and married a nice Jewish medical student. She and Dr. Alan began their family soon after he established his practice on Long

Island, and it was at this moment that Betty initiated her rebellion. There would be no guilt in their home if she could help it. Guilt, in Betty's understanding, was associated with observance, Jewish schools, and the Yiddish language. Her kids would go to public school and learn French as a second language.

Betty, like many of us, was unable to eradicate from her upbringing the unexamined attitudes she had absorbed. Because she had never examined those attitudes, Betty hardly even knew they were there and so she unthinkingly bequeathed them to her children. With a thousand sighs and untold numbers of incessant adages, she conveyed to Zoe and her younger brother, Saul, the basics of her philosophy on life.

The first lesson was this: "The Orthodox will make you crazy with their laws and you don't have to do all that. That's why we moved to Long Island!" Thus the epicenter of the family Jewish custom became the local deli. The second lesson, one not limited to children of the Holocaust but just as easily passed down by family members who experienced the Depression or other economic hardships or challenges, was this: "Life is hard. If you are feeling pleasure from life, you are probably not taking it seriously enough, and God knows life is serious." The result? Betty constantly alternated small indulgences with small denials of pleasure and overlaid both choices with guilt. Is it any wonder that the Zoes of the world grow up confused about pleasure?

Our Double Standards Toward Pleasure

As with so many of the unexamined presumptions concerning pleasure that are floating around, contemporary culture seems to suffer from a collective schizophrenia. On the one hand, we have the vague sense that it is wrong to indulge in too much pleasure. Supersweet chocolate confections are marketed as "devilishly" delicious or "wickedly" decadent. Doesn't sound virtuous. High-school history lessons about the self-destruction of hedonistic cultures linger in the memory as a warning about excess in pleasure. One result of this is that old-fashioned, religious self-righteousness has been replaced by a new, healthier-than-thou smugness. Punctiliousness in eating habits has become the modern benchmark of virtue, and eschewing burgers, fries, MSG, and white rice are signs of political correctness. In this vital campaign, we've been able to count on the moral leadership of no less than a mayor of New York and First Lady of the United States.

On the other hand, just as we get ready to apply this admirable moderation to our sexual habits, we suddenly remember that we've been liberated from self-restriction and are free to indulge in any sexual pleasure we wish. Today the suggestion that some kinds of sex are inherently self-destructive sounds like nosy interference. The suggestion that self-restriction may be beneficial sounds like downright Victorian prudery. What is it in us that will submit to laws about soda sizes and fat content in food but will scream in protest when someone suggests that even an admittedly unhealthy sexual practice ought to be curtailed? Why is our knee-jerk reaction usually outrage: Who do they think they are to tell us how to live our private lives and what pleasures we ought to permit ourselves?

Perhaps the reason we can afford this double standard toward our pleasures is that while today we have the fairly effective means to overcome pregnancy, we haven't found a method to habitually overeat and not get fat. If we had a way to indulge in culinary excess and afterward purge ourselves of the effects, we might jettison self-discipline there as well. Meanwhile, we condone sexual unrestraint but condemn dietary unrestraint—so much so that we are ready to criminalize it.

Unrestrained sexual practice no longer carries the price tag it once did now that we have reliable means to thwart pregnancy and as long as we are reasonably careful to avoid disease. In the past, such unrestraint was potentially socially expensive and was therefore confined mostly to marriage. And it was expected that a pregnancy was likely to occur from engaging in it. Of course, birth control has always been an option and many married couples have tried to limit the number of pregnancies their marriages produce. The difference between birth control of old and modern birth control is that before we had the pill, the IUD, and the diaphragm, the most reliable methods were those that regulated the act itself—that is, partners had to avoid certain times of the month in order to prevent pregnancy. The bottom line was that the use of birth control, at the moment those means were used, was laden with awareness of a baby's imminent possibility.

That is not the case in our time. Our social chatter, our media, our literature, and our behavior provide incontrovertible evidence of a dramatic and deep disconnect between the act of intimacy and the possibility of conceiving a child. The default mode for all sexual behavior now is "protected sex," which while it refers to protection against disease also implies and includes protection against pregnancy. In other words, nowadays in the normal course of events a baby is not supposed to happen.

An ob-gyn, for instance, will ask a woman at her annual checkup which birth control method she is using—not "*Are* you using birth control?" but "*Which* birth control are you using?" Accidents can happen, but they can also be "cleaned up" the morning after, and negligence in "cleaning up" an accident can still be redressed in the early months of pregnancy with an abortion.

Such euphemistic language and the thinking behind it have so removed the idea of an actual physical baby from the pleasures of sex that it truly seems an irrelevance. And a couple who has made the brave move to venture into the zone of "unprotected sex" says demurely to friends, "We are trying to have a baby."

In other words, now they are really trying. Before, they didn't really try. So during all the other times, what were they trying to do?

Their answer would likely be "We were trying to enjoy ourselves. We were after the pleasure." There is a curious anesthetic quality to this preoccupation with pleasure, because those engaged in it are asleep to the fact that, all the time they were concentrating on pleasure, their two physical bodies were trying to make a baby and kept getting thwarted. Meanwhile, their souls wanted to create another soul, but the spiritual energy generated by their union was not able to express itself in the physical body of a baby.

The Pleasure That Takes Us Beyond Ourselves

The contemporary paradigm, then, is that the sexual act is all about pleasure—and what's a baby got to do with it? But in the world outside of our minds—in the world of the uterus, the fertilization of an egg, the biological imperative, and the psychic and spiritual needs to create children—it's *all* about the baby and the real question is "What's pleasure got to do with it?"

Well, in actuality *pleasure has everything to do with it.* There is, of course, no way for a couple to make a baby without pleasure (except by resorting to the test tube), and this act is, without a doubt, intensely physically pleasurable. No other function, no other impulse, no other energy that humans are capable of can produce a baby. Even love can't produce a baby. No matter how much a man loves a woman, his love by itself won't get her pregnant. The two need to participate in this pleasurable activity if they want to conceive a baby.

Isn't it fascinating that a baby is created through an act of pleasure? After all, it didn't have to be like this. Once God decided that there were to be babies in the world, he could have chosen any method at all to make that happen. He could have determined that a husband and wife who wanted a baby would simply sit together and think about a baby and that the baby would be created from this special thought process. For some reason, God instead chose this intensely private activity—an activity that is powered by pleasure—to create a child. In fact, Judaism teaches that the more pleasure a couple experiences in creating a baby, the healthier the baby will be.[1]

Why is this so? And what is it about pleasure that makes it essential to the creation of a baby? If we can understand why the creation of a baby is intrinsically connected to pleasure, we will be in a position to understand how a husband and a wife can achieve true intimacy. Put another way, understanding what true intimacy is lets us also understand why pleasure is such a big part of it.

While physical pleasure is intrinsic to the intimate experience of a husband and a wife, it is not the core pleasure of the intimate experience. As you've seen, the ideal and the core of a man's masculinity is to give. Giving and being received constitute the ultimate pleasure he can achieve. For a woman, the core of her femininity is to receive. When this happens the way it is supposed to, she experiences the ultimate pleasure. In the truly intimate experience, when a husband gives himself unreservedly and the wife gives herself unreservedly, no boundaries remain between them. The ecstasy they experience derives from the awareness of each other and the privilege of becoming one.

Ecstasy is the climax of some sort of stimulation, and there are all types of ecstasies that are the result of various pleasures. The intense pleasure of listening to a musical composition can stir a sensitive soul to rapture-like ecstasy. Intense intellectual concentration and apprehension of a concept can lead to a sort of intellectual ecstasy. Revelation of a transcendent truth can provoke spiritual ecstasy. Some folks are prone to emotional ecstasy, not all of it good. All of these kinds of ecstasy are characterized by the quality of transcendence. In the moment of ecstasy, we go beyond ourselves. We are so focused on the experience of pleasure that all other functions cease. If the ecstatic experience could be reduced to mere words, it might go something like this: *At this moment, I am no longer just me; I am partaking of something beyond my limitations and I am taken out of myself.*

Within the intimacy of a relationship, losing our sense of self is, paradoxically, exhilarating. The border between *being*, that is, being alive and aware of our self, and *not being*, where the self is lost and we are only aware of what is beyond ourselves, brings us to the very border between life and death. At that point, we have stopped caring about ourselves. We have transcended the self. And when we have done so, the creation of a new life becomes possible.

If we are preoccupied with ourselves, there is little room for a baby amid our self-absorption. The ecstasy of intimacy can make a baby because the pleasure in which we lose ourselves creates a space in which the baby can come to be. The very fact that the husband and wife "lose themselves" in this pleasure is what makes the creation of a human being possible.

Pleasure is the essence of the human soul—deeper than the intellect, deeper than emotions, and even deeper than will. Most pleasures take us deeper into the self as we seek even more gratification of our senses. There is, however, another possibility—the opportunity of tapping into a pleasure that is greater than the self and the senses, a pleasure that leads outward from the self. That type of pleasure is the ultimate goal in intimacy. The guidelines that Jewish tradition provides serve to help us achieve that goal, their main point being to clear away distractions that waylay or detour us from this end.

The Real Task of Intimacy

Today distractions abound like never before. While almost any sexual practice one might think of has been around for thousands of years, what is different now is the way in which sex in its myriad variations and expressions smacks us in the face on a daily basis. Incrementally, those images and messages build a mountain of persuasion. What are they trying to persuade us of? That almost any behavior is acceptable, that the most adventurous among us will dabble in most of it, and that only the uptight deny themselves the pleasure of trying out unusual practices.

By the time a child has waded through eighteen years of exposure to this stuff, he or she knows how to do it all. Yet these young people aren't taught even the first thing about having a healthy life of intimacy with one another. What's worse is that whatever they do know, whatever they have learned, is distracting. It's exactly the wrong guidance for achieving true intimacy because the education they receive focuses exclusively on self-gratification.

Using optimum physical pleasure, the "ultimate orgasm," as a yardstick to measure each sexual encounter is dispiriting, for it invites evaluation of the performance. Husband and wife ask one another, "Was it good enough?" In other words, the physical pleasure of the act has become an end in itself (which is, in effect, what we consider pornography.)

When that is the case, when the goal is the physical pleasure of the act itself rather than shared intimacy laden with pleasure, it is as if a third participant is present and interposed between the two people. They are not becoming one through intimacy; they are sharing a third enterprise. They're not directly experiencing each other; they are experiencing the pleasure of the act, like enjoying a good movie together or going biking together. The pleasure has become a garment between them. It divides rather than unites them.

All the while that we pursue the false ambition for optimum physical pleasure, an ambition that will never satisfy us, we are numbing ourselves so that we don't feel our real needs. It's like the analogy you read about earlier—trying to assuage hunger with junk food. As long as we focus on outward pleasures, we are going to be ignoring the real need, the deep need of every soul for intimacy. That need never goes away, and that hunger can never be satisfied by mere physical pleasure.

In intimacy, the pleasure will happen all on its own. It doesn't need any help. In intimacy, the real task of a couple is to experience one another directly without separation and without any distractions that could come between them, even the distraction of preoccupation with physical pleasure. The absence of any distraction is the preamble to true intimacy.

Pleasure is an essential element of intimacy, but preoccupation with physical pleasure leads to greater self-absorption and detracts from our shared intimacy. True intimacy takes us beyond ourselves to a pleasure that is greater than the self or the senses.

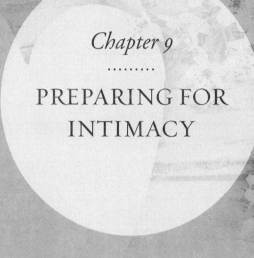

Chapter 9
....
PREPARING FOR
INTIMACY

Preparing for Intimacy

. . . .

THE TWELFTH-CENTURY PHILOSOPHER Maimonides, one of the greatest of all Jewish scholars, taught that in some ways the preparation for an act is more important than the act itself.[1] The reason is this: In our preparations for something, we envision our goal. Doing that is not only the surest method to attaining our goal but often the only way to make sure we get there.

The more important a destination is to us, the more extensive our preparations to get there. We download directions before setting out on a journey. We carefully prepare remarks before speaking in front of a powerful audience. In the same way, if we are going to be practical about achieving success in intimacy—the most emotional and important act of our marriage—we must prepare ourselves for it. Intimacy is at the heart of a marriage, so getting it right is absolutely vital. Preparation puts our mind where it needs to be and reminds us of where we want to end up.

The idea of preparation for intimacy rankles a lot of people. Debby attended a talk I gave on this subject and her reaction, like that of almost everyone else in the class, was initially contentious. Debby believed that the real excitement in an intimate encounter lay in its spontaneity. To Debby, intimacy was, above all else, an expression of emotion, fired up spontaneously by the circumstances of the moment.

She was not alone in this opinion. Judging by the reactions of others in the class, most of them concurred that intimacy is at its best when it has been least prepared for, when it is unexpected. Preparation would spoil the game, they believed. The entire idea of preparation for intimacy seemed to work against what they considered to be the most stimulating element of the sexual experience—that sense of urgent need that must be answered immediately, wherever one might be. The male members of the class in particular insisted that urgency, the unwillingness to delay for even a moment one's desire, demonstrated attraction and passion. They were positive that this kind of heated spontaneity was as exciting for their wives as it was for them.

While Debby was listening to the men make their case, she began to rethink her own experiences. She realized that, if she was being honest with herself, her enthusiasm for this type of impulsive act had been at least partially feigned. In fact, if she was excited by it at all, it was because it was exciting for her partner, not because it excited her directly. The truth was that it often felt unwelcome.

In general, most men don't need emotional involvement to summon arousal. For them, the process requires a minimum of encouragement. The problems crop up when men make the mistake of believing that women are the same as they are in this regard. Not only are women not like men, but a woman's path toward sexual stimulation is completely different from that of a man. A woman craves emotional involvement when she is with her husband. When that's not there, she feels hollow, even if she has experienced so-called "sexual satisfaction." By reconsidering the contributions of each partner, we can understand the difference between men and women more clearly.

What a Woman Needs

On a purely biological level, a man provides a life-giving force during intimacy. His contribution fertilizes and makes the growth of life possible. It shouldn't be and usually isn't difficult for him to sense how he is needed. When it comes to a woman, while her participation is no less obvious, defining her exact role requires more subtle understanding. What she provides in this experience is a home, a space to receive life. What she needs during intimacy is to know that her husband acknowledges that and appreciates her for her unique role. Her need is a bit more complicated because appreciation needs to be communicated. A woman needs kind words and thoughtful actions to justify her surrender.

Men sometimes think the time invested in that is off topic, but it's not. Appreciating and giving tender care to his partner is the way for a man to get where he wants to go. Maimonides says that a husband should begin intimacy by using words that will "draw his wife's heart to him."[2] This refers not to sexually charged words but to words of love and appreciation that are spoken even before they get to the bedroom.

Someone in the class suggested that all this planning and preparation made intimacy sound calculated, stiff, and dispassionate and, as such, was decidedly unromantic. I disagreed. Romance is about being creative and innovative in a relationship. For example, we consider a man who spends time and effort thinking up and carrying out an elaborate scheme for proposing marriage as "romantic." Nothing elaborate is required to be romantic on an ongoing basis. The simple act of bringing home flowers is romantic. A small gift is romantic. Words of love are romantic. Still, most gestures and actions that we term "romantic," as simple as they may be, involve some sort of contemplation beforehand. They are anything but spontaneous. The kind of spontaneity the people in the class were talking about began to sound like a byword for speed, which for many women tends to cool rather than build passion.

"You can put a vehicle in drive and hit the accelerator," I said, "but if you have no idea where you want to go, what is the point?" Someone in the class replied, to great laughter, "Who cares? It's exciting to just go. It's all about the journey." That's a slogan to slap on a Facebook page, but many people have neither the time, stamina, or desire to set off on an emotional journey at high speed with no clue as to the destination. For most of us, that's frankly a little scary and we'd rather avoid the risk of crashing.

Bringing All of Yourself to the Experience

What sort of preparations should we make for intimacy? Jewish wisdom contains some helpful guidelines about how a couple should go about setting the best mood for intimacy.[3] These guidelines are aimed at focusing the energies of the husband and wife in such a way that they are wholly present in the experience. Here are some examples.

First, a couple should not be together if one of them is angry. The reason? Anger compels the mind and heart of the one who is angry to be preoccupied with distracting thoughts or emotions, to be focused somewhere else than on the intimate moment. For intimacy to take place, differences have to be resolved and peace regained.

Another example is that we should not be intimate with our spouse out of a drive for conquest or out of spite, because the enjoyment of the act is then motivated by a desire for victory or revenge rather than a desire for intimacy. Similarly, if one spouse is drunk, the couple should not be together because intoxicants impair our minds and make us incapable of focusing on the reality of the intimacy.

In addition, during intimate moments together each partner should try not to think about anything else. If a woman's mind is still on the question of which contractor to hire to do the renovations on the basement, she is bringing to her spouse only half her heart and a mostly absent mind.[4]

It's also best to eliminate any other detracting excitements that might add to the pleasure but not to the pleasure of intimacy. For instance, if a couple is not in their own home and the door of the room they are in has no lock on it, the possibility exists of someone barging in. That risk may add an element of thrill to their togetherness, but that pleasure is not the pleasure of intimacy. In fact, that risk degrades the intimacy because the couple cannot fully concentrate on the intimate experience.

Of course, it goes without saying that during sexual intercourse one should not be thinking about someone other than one's spouse. So important are the thoughts that accompany our actions that Judaism considers having thoughts about a stranger during sex as akin to adultery. Also, intimacy cannot truly occur if either partner has decided to get divorced. The intimate act requires a total union of mind and body, with both spouses wholly present and completely focused. If they are thinking of leaving the marriage, how can they achieve any union, any oneness? The lesson we can take away from all these examples is that *when a couple removes all things that separate them, oneness comes naturally.*

One more key that opens the door to intimacy, perhaps the most important, is the presence of joy. When people are miserable or depressed, they are almost incapable of pleasure. Delicious food is wasted on them; they don't appreciate it. Alcohol may be an attractive anesthetic to someone who is miserable, but it might as well be cheap wine as the finest champagne. Taste doesn't matter and isn't noticed when all you are trying to do is numb yourself.

To truly appreciate and absorb pleasure, it is best to experience it when you are already happy. Some mistakenly think intimacy in itself will fill a void, making them happy when they are feeling down. It's a mistake to believe that partaking of sexual pleasure will alleviate loneliness, alienation, or depression.

To turn things around in your personal life and in your relationship, start by working to make your own life more joyful, infusing it with more meaning. I am not making light of the real challenges we all face. But attempting to use sex or pleasure of any sort to self-medicate is only avoiding the core issues underlying the pain. It just doesn't work.

The point here is that bringing happiness to the act of intimacy heightens the pleasure. The buoyancy of joy is part of the preparation for the intimate act. And what's not to be happy about? When a husband and a wife are intimate, they experience transcendence in their relationship that isn't possible in any other aspect of their lives. That encounter is sacred and the experience of it colors their entire marriage in all its aspects. It brings nourishment and spiritual health to their union that spreads out to the whole family.

*Preparing for intimacy
enhances the experience.
By clearing away all distractions,
a husband and wife can concentrate fully
on each other, inviting oneness
to come naturally.*

Chapter 10

....

ARE WE
ALONE YET?

Are We Alone Yet?

. . . .

THE TECHNOLOGY THAT governs modern life, from smartphones and iPods to laptops and tablets, creates a cacophony that is proving more and more difficult to retreat from. Ever-increasing diversions, distractions, and demands make their appearance instantaneously anywhere, anytime. With all that happening around us, forging a focused and meaningful relationship that we can pour our energy into seems an elusive possibility. Instead of being able to spend quality time sharing our deepest thoughts and convictions with another person, we find ourselves more fragmented, alone, and alienated than ever.

Josh, whom you met in chapter 3, experienced alienation repeatedly—most recently in his failed marriage. He craved a deep, intimate connection but could never find it. Finally, he came to believe that there was something wrong inside of him that barred him from finding a woman he could share that kind of deep relationship with.

In reality, the issue wasn't that he was somehow hopelessly flawed. The problem had to do with the marital life he and his wife had built—or rather, failed to build—together. When he finally realized this, he was sad about the missed opportunities of the past, but he was buoyed by the thought that he could change his behavior and thereby the outcome of any new relationship. Individuals like Josh often express the belief that they are hopeless where love and marriage are concerned. Learning that they can actually discover another way of being married gives them hope.

Josh had also come to see privacy as an important factor at the heart of intimacy. He wasn't wrong about that, but privacy by itself does not provide all that intimacy needs. The word *modesty* is a more appropriate and comprehensive way of describing how we can ensure a deep, intimate relationship. You read in chapter 4 that modest behavior is a way to protect and preserve our natural intimate responses in preparation for a healthy intimate life. Modesty also has another dimension, which we'll explore here—one that helps us bring an attitude of sacredness to the bedroom.

Not that long ago, what went on in the bedroom of a married couple was not spoken about in polite society. In the 1950s and 1960s, networks banned TV shows from showing married couples in the same bed. If we saw them in their bedrooms at all, they were in separate beds. People did not publicly refer to the pregnancy bumps that were visual confirmation of an active marital life. When Lucille Ball became pregnant while starring in *I Love Lucy*, her character, Lucy Ricardo, was scripted into the show as waiting for a baby. All the shows until the baby was born were taped without anyone ever uttering the word *pregnant*, using instead what the producers felt were more acceptable euphemisms.

Eighty years ago, if a fourteen-year-old asked her grandmother what went on in a married couple's bedroom, the answer would probably have been "nothing." Nothing? Really? Who was Grandma trying to kid? What was the point of such apparent prudery? Perhaps when Grandma said "nothing," she was not merely being evasive but conveying a deeper truth—a truth hinted at in the word *mezuzah*.

The Power of "No Thing"

Affixed to each doorway in a Jewish dwelling is a *mezuzah*, a scroll of parchment inscribed with the words of the Shema (a passage from the Book of Deuteronomy containing the central proclamation of faith—that "God is One"). The scroll is rolled up tightly and covered, fixed upon the upper third of the right doorpost, and customarily touched and kissed as one enters the room. Jewish wisdom teaches that having a *mezuzah* on each door protects the home.

The Hebrew spelling of the word *mezuzah* can be separated into three parts: the Hebrew letters *mem,* implying harmony; *zu,* meaning "this" in its masculine form, implying "him"; and *zah,* meaning "this" in its feminine form, implying "her." That tells us that the home (including the bedroom), with the *mezuzah* affixed on the doorposts, embraces "him" and "her" in graceful harmony. That means that in our home, marriage, and family life, we embrace and share more than "things"; we share ourselves.

Today the concept of "things" is something we must all grapple with. It's easy to imagine all sorts of dangers we need protection from, but a harmful influence we often forget to protect against is the whole concept of "things" and the role they've come to assume in our lives. In looking at the world with the eyes of a consumer, the biggest risk we run is reducing even the people in our lives to objects. It is distressingly easy for our egos to snare us into seeing our children, our friends, our family, and our spouses as means to some personal end. That attitude, often so subtle that we are not aware of it, wears away at our relationships, causing cracks and stress points.

Nowhere is that subtle attitude more corrosive than in the marital bedroom. That is why nothing—*no thing*—should be brought by the couple into the sacred space of the bedroom. At the moment of intimacy, *no thing* should be there with a wife and husband, not even one element that could distract from their union.

Creating a Sacred Space

For a generation raised with a casual attitude toward sex, it may be surprising to learn that the Jewish tradition likens the marital bedroom to a holy place, in this case to the Holy of Holies of the Temple in Jerusalem.[1] In the center of the Temple there was a chamber called the Holy (the *Kodesh*), where priests attended to various daily tasks, and beyond it was the Holy of Holies (the *Kodesh HaKadoshim*), which was off-limits to everyone. The Holy of Holies was God's space, endowed with unique spiritual energy, and the one who entered it had to be worthy of that space. On only one day of the year, Yom Kippur, the High Priest alone was allowed into this space and for no more time than it took him to complete the special offering for Yom Kippur—less than a half hour all told. When he finished this ritual, he retreated from the room until the same season the next year.

In the Holy Land that is marriage, the bedroom, where a husband and wife are intimate, is a dwelling place for the presence of God. Here the couple comes together as one, affirming the mystery of creation. Here a couple creates children, with God as the third partner.[2] Their spiritual energy impacts that space. The material objects within the bedroom absorb the energies created by the intimacy of a husband and a wife and reflect those energies back, endowing the room with holy vitality. Because of its mystical and transformative power, intimacy deserves serious respect. It is sacred.

In a synagogue, the most sacred object is the Torah scroll, upon which is handwritten the text of the Torah. For this reason, the scroll is kept out of sight in a curtained cabinet and removed only when it is going to be read. The scroll is sheltered behind a curtain out of respect for its sanctity—precisely the principle upon which the privacy of the marital bedroom is based. In other words, intimacy is holy, and everything we do in connection with it must be respectful and mindful of the modesty needed to shelter and nurture it.

The attitude of sacredness and privacy that we bring to intimacy is another way of understanding the concept of modesty. External modesty has to do with how we speak, act, behave, interact with others, and dress. There is also an internal modesty. On a personal level, internal modesty has to do with allowing your inner thoughts and feelings to remain private. As a couple, that kind of modesty means that your private life together remains private, and the expression of your inner feelings for each other stays between the two of you, protected within the circle of your oneness.

Being Fully Present

To be intimate, a husband and wife must know they are completely alone. They create a sacrosanct space and time that are inviolable and impregnable, where only the two enter and where no other factors or influences are present. Nothing besides the two of them. Their intimacy begins the moment they enter the bedroom, for that entrance states intention.

Because this is a private act, nothing the husband and wife say or do before or after should telegraph news of it to anyone else. When intimacy is going to take place, the husband initiates the act. In the Jewish tradition, it is considered praiseworthy for the wife not to demand intimacy or to ask for it explicitly but to send her husband modest "signals" of invitation.[3] As noted before, her womb, her openness, invites him to lead them in this dance. Once begun, this activity is holier than any other activity a couple can do together. Indeed, the Talmud asserts that when a married couple is unified in the intimate act, God is present with them.[4]

The sages have proposed many suggestions to keep couples focused and to assist them in achieving what amounts to a sublime awareness. Note that these are suggestions, not requirements; for according to Jewish law, a married couple is actually permitted to do almost anything in their intimate time together.[5] Most of the suggestions seek to encourage and support concentration, assisting husband and wife to be completely tuned in to what is happening to the exclusion of everything else. Here are some of them.

It's best that nothing be present that will interfere with a couple's concentration—no TV or computer in the room, no music playing to distract the couple with lyrics or melody. The two of them are not concerned about others because their discretion has insured that no one knows what they are doing. As mentioned earlier, it's also important to clear out negative thoughts and to avoid intimacy when either partner is experiencing insobriety, anger, or thoughts of separation.

Certainly, there should be no pornography. Pornography, of course, is problematic on many levels. For one, it turns the one who should be our most cherished friend and lover into simply an object to be treated impersonally and mechanically. It causes tragic wreckage of its participants' lives. In a married couple's bedroom, it is particularly damaging. Pornography injects other people into their sacred space. It objectifies the act itself, turning it into a thing and making true intimacy impossible.

If we are fortunate, we will have decades of happiness in our marriage, even as we meet all manner of vicissitudes together. Much of the power to bring about that happiness is in our hands. If we approach our marriage with reverence and if we protect it from all sides with modesty, we will help to create a home that is filled with light, love, and sanctity.

*Reverence for one's spouse is
an essential ingredient of intimacy.
We foster intimacy by creating
a sacred space in the bedroom
and being fully present
with each other.*

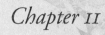

Chapter 11
....

THE
MYTH OF SEX AS
ENTERTAINMENT

The Myth of
Sex as Entertainment

. . . .

TOLSTOY WROTE, "Happy families are all alike; every unhappy family is unhappy in its own way." Then he went on to explore the vicissitudes of one unhappy family that, like so many others, was having problems with sex. That is the stone that trips up many marriages; and, in most cases, when a couple stumbles on it their intimate life together also comes to a halt.

Many marriages come crashing to the ground because of apathy. How do we account for a lack of interest in such a basic human activity as sex? Animals, as long as they are physically capable, never lose interest. After all, "birds do it, bees do it / even educated fleas do it."[1] Surely, from the simple physical attraction of one body to another, it doesn't make sense that a couple should ever lose interest.

The crux of the problem seems to be that we have replaced a profoundly simple understanding of intimacy—that a married couple comes together to share and unite—with a confusing perception that sex is entertainment. And, as with any form of entertainment, we eventually grow bored with it.

The Bait and Switch That Leads to Nonfulfillment

The myth that sex is entertainment is something I discussed at a couples retreat in Miami that Josh showed up for. He told me he was a bit embarrassed to be the only single man present and had even toyed with the idea of pretending he had a wife sick with the flu upstairs in their hotel room. Sitting in the conference room, Josh was hearing some of the same lessons he had already absorbed but with a new spin. It turned out that waking up to the truth that sex was more than simply a form of entertainment was an important stepping-stone for Josh.

At the retreat, I spoke of how modesty and privacy are essential to creating intimacy. Those attending complained about the difficulties of creating a roped-off private area of intimacy in their lives. Josh, like many of those present, also felt that it was almost impossible to escape society's incessant reinforcement of sex as entertainment.

In the public world around us, the portrayal of sex as entertainment is everywhere all the time. It sells everything from drinks to cars. It fuels industries from music to medicine. Our politicians and statesmen regularly entertain us by engaging in titillating, sometimes ridiculous situations that sell newspapers and sway public opinion. Many children learned for the first time about oral sex in connection with the behavior of a recent president of the United States and they continue to pick up other such "tips" all the time. As they plod through the PG-13 movies of their adolescence, they continue to amass information about methods and alternatives. In short, they are gaining an education in how to use their bodies to entertain themselves.

After twenty or more years of absorbing everything that modern culture can impart on this subject, young people get married and drag all this information into their bedrooms with them. Because everybody assumes that a successful married life hinges on variety in the bedroom, they learn many different methods, positions, and practices to use with their spouses. It's a common belief that diversity of stimulation and methods staves off boredom and prevents apathy in a marriage. Conventional wisdom has it that a bored spouse is more apt to wander off and look elsewhere for satisfaction and that the way to keep your spouse interested and roped in is to keep him or her entertained. But is that true?

The reality is that an appetite for variety, once installed as the standard for making choices in the bedroom, is insatiable. We will always seek fresh stimulation, and we can never get enough variety to satisfy our appetite. So rather than preventing dissatisfaction, variety ultimately leads to it.

As Josh and those attending the retreat began to understand, a bait-and-switch con job is at work here. When a couple takes the bait of sex as entertainment, they may not realize for quite some time, perhaps not until it is too late, that they have traded the satisfaction of intimacy for the continual stimulation of physical organs. That approach actually shackles a couple within their physical bodies, forestalling the pleasure of an experience beyond those limitations. Eventually, most people will feel this lack, perhaps as a sense of loneliness, emptiness, or nonfulfillment, although they may never know why they feel that way.

Achieving More than a Physical Climax

Intimacy is pleasurable; no one would want it otherwise. The suggestions you've read about in previous chapters and the ones you'll read about here are meant to help couples successfully navigate around the temptation of small pleasures in order to gain the incomparably greater pleasure of true intimacy. The basic purpose of these guidelines is to bring about a sharply focused and intensely spiritual, not just physical, climax. As you've seen, one thing we can do to help accomplish this is to close out sensory distractions that could drain away the strength of the excitement to peripheral or secondary pleasures.

Take the example of visual distraction. On the one hand, what the eye sees stimulates the person, and the stimulation is often pleasurable. Nakedness is notoriously stimulating. Becoming preoccupied with this vision, however, is a distraction. Dwelling on another's physicality, no matter how admiringly, precludes us from going further in gaining deeper knowledge of our partner—and we would much rather be known than seen.

We may think of this preoccupation as something that happens in encounters between strangers, but it can happen with our spouse too. If we focus primarily on seeing the body, we stall the journey into further knowledge and deeper intimacy. The eye can only see things about a person but never the person. You can stare at a person for a year and not know who that person is. You can see what he is—tall, short, fat, skinny— but that doesn't mean you'll *know* the person. (The same is true, by the way, in our relationship with God. We want to draw closer to him, but he is not visible. He has made it that way because if we could see him, we would search no further. We would be satisfied with what we have seen—something awesome about him that is not truly him.)

In the intimacy that occurs between a husband and wife, they are each surrendering but to something greater than the two of them. At that moment, intimacy surrounds both of them and embraces them, turning them into one being. That intimacy cannot be seen. Whatever we see inevitably becomes a distraction from real intimacy. That is why it's best for intimacy to occur in the dark. Then the encounter unfolds in such a way that the couple is not distracted by any sight, including the sight of each other.[2]

This is a good place to talk about a myth that sometimes gets bandied about—that Jewish couples must use a sheet with a hole to accomplish their union. That myth probably arose out of the same mysterious swamp that the myth that Jews have horns emerged from. The fact is that, according to Jewish law, the couple must be completely naked, for there should be nothing between a husband and a wife when they are together. Nothing. Even clothing can be a distraction.

What Encourages and Inhibits Intimacy

Any practice in the bedroom that inhibits real intimacy or, worse yet, is aimed at avoiding actual union is problematic. Part of the reason couples avoid union, and it happens frequently, is that so many people who don't want to have babies are having sex. Part of the training young people get during their teen years teaches them, sometimes rather explicitly in school, that whatever cannot get a person pregnant, the so-called "outercourse," is preferable. The message is that the real thing is dangerous, so try this other stuff. If one uses hands or mouth, it's safer, easier, and usually quicker.

It's also much more shallow. It certainly doesn't bring two people closer, nor does it bring them to intimacy. In fact, it doesn't make much sense. In the end, hands and mouths are not intimate organs; they are cheats. They come up seriously short as substitutes for the real thing, the adult stuff that risks true intimacy.

Another practice that leads us away from union is masturbation, both male and female. There's an old joke about masturbation that "you don't meet many interesting people that way." Ultimately, masturbation is detrimental for that very reason—it is spectacular self-absorption. It leads one inward toward oneself and away from union and intimacy. Any sort of behavior on the way to intercourse that allows or encourages self-absorption will inevitably erode a sense of union.

Intimacy is ultimately about vulnerability, a vulnerability that brings about the temporary abandonment of separate egos. For such an awesome encounter, it's recommended that during actual union husband and wife be face to face, although they do not have to see eye to eye.[3] In addition, each of them should ideally face the source from which he or she was created—the husband facing the earth from which Adam was created and the wife facing her husband, as the woman was taken from the man.[4]

Facing one another during actual intercourse makes possible both a kiss and an embrace. A kiss is intensely intimate. The mingling of breath that occurs with a kiss demonstrates that the closeness of intimacy is more than just the closeness of two bodies; it is a mingling of spirit. The embrace of a husband and wife is uniquely human and expresses our spiritual makeup. Animals don't need to face one another because there is no soul in the other that they need to reach out to. A husband and wife, though, are "knowing" one another and theirs is a soul-to-soul encounter.

Admittedly, some of these suggestions may seem daunting and it will not always be possible, even in a good marriage, to constantly remain on such an ideal level of awareness. For this reason, Judaism is eminently practical. Though it recommends a high bar of behavior, it permits a husband and wife almost any type of foreplay as part of their intimate encounters. A husband should do whatever he can to help his wife achieve physical gratification during intimacy, and both should avoid what is distasteful or uncomfortable to either one of them.[5]

At the moment of climax, it is ideal for the thoughts of a couple to be centered on what unites them. Nothing would be more appropriate than to think at that time of affecting another life through their intimacy, the life of a baby. Since such primacy is placed on the creation of a baby in the intimate act, couples commonly ask what happens when intimacy cannot result in a baby. Should husband and wife refrain from intimacy when it's not possible for them to create a baby? The answer is no.

Even if a couple is not going to have a child—if, for example, the wife is already pregnant or cannot conceive or the couple is too old for babies—it is still important for the husband and wife to share intimacy.[6] Why? Because the spiritual effects of intimacy hold true even if a physical baby will not or cannot be created.[7] The psychological and emotional truths of intimacy are no less important in those circumstances. A couple's intimacy can still have a spiritual effect on other lives.

Indeed, the mystical teachings of Kabbalah say that a husband and wife can affect other souls during their union. That is why the Torah declares that at the moment of intimate union between a husband and wife, God is present, dwelling between them. The spiritual radiance from their act of union spills over to have a spiritual effect that goes well beyond themselves.[8]

*Sex and intimacy are more than
a form of entertainment. Intimacy is
an encounter between two souls and can
bring about not just a physical but a
spiritually pleasurable climax.*

~

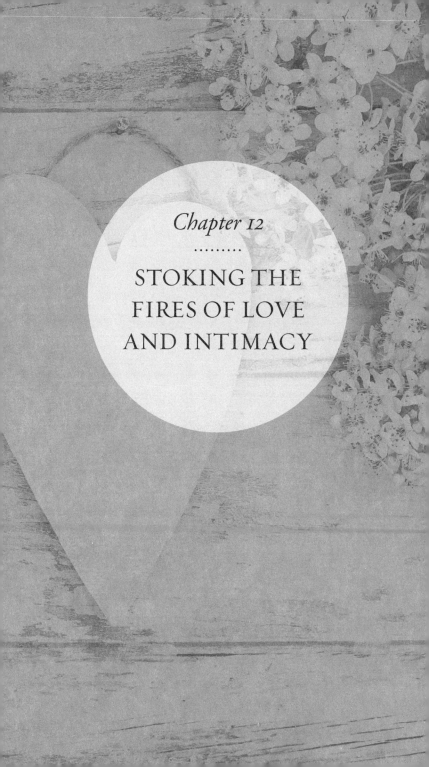

Chapter 12

·········

STOKING THE
FIRES OF LOVE
AND INTIMACY

Stoking the Fires
of Love and Intimacy

. . . .

IN *FIDDLER ON THE ROOF*, Tevye asks his wife, Golde, "Do you love me?" Golde responds, "Do I what?" And Tevye repeats, "Do you love me?" Golde lists all the ways she has taken care of her husband and shared his life for the past twenty-five years. "If that's not love, what is?" she concludes.

What *is* love? Of course, there are going to be problems defining that word when we use it to describe both our feelings for a spouse of twenty-five years and the feelings we have for a hot fudge sundae. If we want to understand more clearly what love really is, we need to investigate and reformulate the language we use.

Most of us have experienced the love that is found in family relationships—father and son, mother and daughter, brother and sister. These relationships are grounded in nature and reflect an innate love that may well be an extension of the love we have for ourselves. The participants are connected from the start, born with a bond to one another. The love in those kinds of relationships is steady, reassuring, and constant. It thrives on familiarity and consistency. Its very predictability is what makes it so comforting and why we treasure it so much. The close bonds that exist within families is also why family conflict has such a keen impact upon us and why conflict among family members can feel as disruptive as conflict within oneself.

The love between a husband and a wife is different than the love between family members. Essentially, a husband and wife are strangers from different planets. They come from different environments, meet, and then begin a life together. Tomorrow they could divorce and walk away from each other and once again they would no longer belong to one another. No matter how long a couple is married and no matter how close and loving they become, they remain mysteriously different even after twenty-five years. That natural distance between them is a spiritual divide they must continually bridge. It will never go away—and that's actually a good thing.

Here's why. Because of the divide between husband and wife, the love they feel toward one another is not a calm love like the love we share with a brother or sister. Married love is fiery, passionate, and intense. It is not constant; it flares up and cools down again. That's what makes it unique and what creates the attraction. The strength of this kind of love lies in the fact that it is *not* constant and consistent. Were the relationship of husband and wife to become steady and unchanging like that of a brother and sister, the relationship would become stagnant, and that would be unhealthy.

Leaping across the Divide

The natural psychic distance between a husband and wife creates the desire to close the space between them, to leap across the divide. This leap is fueled by fiery love, which in turn stokes the love with more intensity. Marriage thrives on this. Intimacy depends on the awareness that our spouse is a separate being and that to reach him or her, we must leap across a divide. Thus, distance not only makes the heart grow fonder; it also makes the heart grow more passionate.

The most deadly attitude we can encounter in marriage is familiarity, a truth captured in the aphorism "familiarity breeds contempt." More than that, familiarity threatens intimacy. Underlying the attitude of familiarity is a sense of entitlement. Familiarity's claim is that this is territory we are allowed to enter at will. When we take someone for granted, intimacy is no longer given, no longer shared as a gift from one to another. Instead, we take what we feel entitled to take. The problem is that when we try to seize intimacy, it disappears.

For Debby, learning that the love between family members is quite different than the love between a husband and wife was liberating. Debby, as we've seen, grew up in a home with only her mother, all the while craving the comfort of a sibling and the warmth and secure love of a father. She now realized that with each man she had dated, she had been waiting for their relationship to develop into something that would feel comfortable, warm, and familial.

As it happened, none of the men she had dated wanted to play the role of either brother or father. So she had always been left feeling disappointed, lost, and lonely, ultimately unable to find the man she thought she needed. At last she was able to see that she would never overcome the lack of a sibling by getting married. Nor was she going to find a substitute for her father, marry him, and try to rectify the mistakes of her parents. While Debby felt sad that she would never be able to find what she had lost in childhood, she was relieved to finally understand that marriage was not a way to try to fill the holes in her life.

Gaining self-knowledge is empowering, even when the knowledge is bitter. In Debby's case, her newfound insights equipped her with a desire to try again. She understood that she didn't need a man to become her emotional center. She needed to find her own vision of life and then find a man to share it with. That's what Golde was saying to Tevye when he kept asking her,

"Do you love me?" She was, in essence, saying: "You're asking about one emotion when, in fact, I've given you all of me."

Creating a Healthy Separation

Another two years would pass before Debby met her future fiancé, Avi. During that time, Debby gained a deepening understanding of intimacy. The question she faced as she prepared for her marriage was how to achieve real intimacy and how to sustain it throughout her married life.

How is one to retain the excitement of a new relationship after years of marriage and of living day by day in the same house? After twenty-five years, how is it possible to avoid becoming too familiar with your spouse? Early in marriage, the thrill can seem to come from jumping over the divide between oneself and a stranger. But what kind of a divide can still exist when two people have lived together beneath one roof for years?

One way to keep igniting the spark in a relationship is to recognize and honor the natural rhythm inherent in a marriage—the rhythm of the passionate rush to close a distance followed by a temporary cooling and individuation until one longs to close that distance again. That rhythm is captured and preserved in one of the guidelines the Torah lays down for marriage. It instructs a couple not to be physically intimate during the wife's period and for seven days following the last evidence of menstrual flow.[1]

During the days they have suspended their physical relationship, they do nothing that might hint at or begin intimacy. To create a degree of physical separation between themselves, they do not share a bed. They do not kiss, hold hands, or speak of intimate matters. Intimacy is serious business, and the smallest signals toward it are consequential and should not be undertaken unless intimacy is intended. At the end of the separation period, the wife goes to a ritual bath, called a *mikveh*. She immerses herself in its waters, after which the couple may come together in intimacy.

Such a protocol creates an intentional interlude in intimacy and forces a new and eager couple to develop their relationship on more than physical grounds. Later in life, a husband and wife inevitably come to appreciate the opportunity this monthly time-out affords them to develop emotional and intellectual bonds.

The drawing apart and coming back together again provides a rhythm to married life that mirrors the rhythm between two souls: we are separate, but we reach across a distance to come together. That rhythm stokes the fiery love between a husband and a wife. And the days of suspended physical contact make a couple's renewed intimacy as exciting as though they were at the beginning of their relationship.

Familiarity is deadly to marriage
because it fosters a sense of entitlement
and nonchalance. Leaping across a divide
to come together time and again keeps
a marriage alive and vibrant.

~

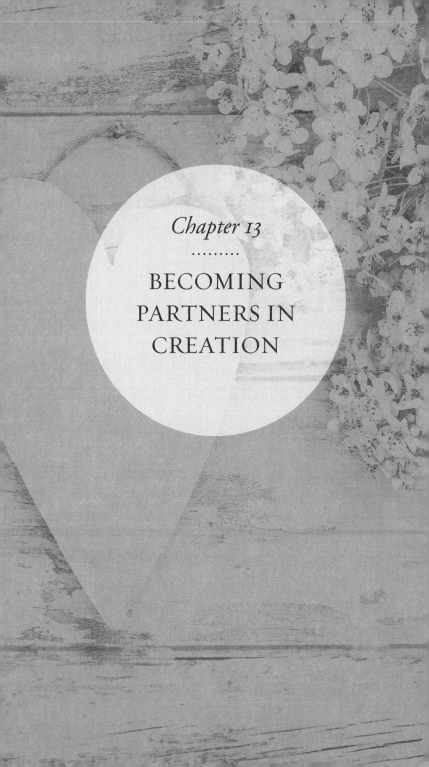

Chapter 13
....

BECOMING
PARTNERS IN
CREATION

Becoming Partners
in Creation

. . . .

AT THE END of the Second World War, as the ashes of the Holocaust began to settle, the displaced persons camps in Europe started to fill with survivors. Most of them were young people, many just out of their teens, and all of them had just witnessed the worst that humans can do to one another. They had seen hell on earth and now found themselves alone. Most were adrift without a single surviving family member.

Some were so traumatized by what they had seen that they found normal life impossible. Whether they had been drained of the desire for a family or the strength to build one, they looked at the mountains of Jewish corpses and had no wish to bring new children into the world. We can understand their despair. What is beyond understanding, what seems miraculous in fact, is that the majority of the young people who survived did go on to find partners, marry, conceive, and raise a new generation.

What mysterious strength was hidden in them? What sort of parents had planted within them the power to do this rebuilding? It's a fascinating question: What kind of parenting is needed to raise a child who can endure a Holocaust and come out at the other end saying, "I am going to start a new family"? What supernatural parenting achieved this? Could we ever hope to raise a generation like this today? Faith, strength, courage, whatever it took—how were those qualities embedded in these young people?

The answer is that no generation raises the next generation all on its own. The Jewish people are the inheritors of five thousand years of holy parenting. What the parents of these Holocaust survivors gave their children did not begin with them; it did not even begin with their grandparents. Generation after generation, Jewish marriages have been sustained by modesty and grace and the wisdom that this is the way to preserve true intimacy, even in the most terrible times.

What does this wisdom compete with nowadays? What is the contemporary model for a family and what examples can young people draw from real life and the society they live in? In the movies, from which many take their cue, the romance always ends when the hero and heroine get together. We don't get to find out how the marriage works out—unless it's a movie about how marriage pretty much doesn't work out. It would be wonderful if today's young adults could learn about marriage from the example of their own parents. Unfortunately, many are not that lucky. According to Furstenberg, Peterson, and Nord, "Half of all children will witness the breakup of a parent's marriage. Of these, close to half will also see the breakup of a parent's second marriage."[1]

We are living in a different universe from the pre-war world that the survivors of the Holocaust were born into. They overcame the worst imaginable circumstances and then, after the maelstrom, went on to restore the civilization they had grown up in—and for the most part, they succeeded. If the children of our society had to restore morality and health to civilization, would they even know what to do? It is a national tragedy that an entire generation has learned little that would equip them for such a job.

Despite fifty years of no-fault divorce and modern media entertainment that has unraveled the tapestry of family life, I believe it is possible to knit that tapestry back together, one family at a time. By applying what we have learned about love, sex, and intimacy, we can create an environment that is conducive to raising morally strong and healthy children. A healthy family begins in the parents' bedroom and holy parenting begins at conception. So becoming aware of the deeper mysteries of what takes place at conception and birth is key if we would practice the transformative power of real intimacy.

What Really Takes Place at Conception

In the years since I first met Zoe and her second husband, David, they had traveled quite a distance together. After a few years of marriage, they told me they had decided to become parents—a decision that took a lot of courage for them. Parenting, in Zoe's experience, had always seemed almost accidental rather than intentional. That attitude stemmed from an experience that had made a big impression on Zoe as a young teenager.

One day when she was about thirteen, Zoe and her friend Clare were visiting Clare's eccentric grandmother. While they were there, Clare's grandmother confessed to the two impressionable girls that of all her five children, the only one she had really wanted had been Clare's uncle, Jonathan. Clare had looked a little chagrined upon hearing that her mother, one of the other four children, had been unwanted. Grandma clarified that Jonathan's pregnancy was the only one that she had planned and that the faulty birth control of the 1950s had misfired four times. That piece of information had colored Zoe's view of children ever since: kids were chaos from the beginning. The entire proposition, from conception through college, seemed to imply a loss of control.

Things were now looking different to Zoe. She had taken to heart and embraced what she had learned about the true nature of intimacy and marriage and about the process of conception and giving birth. What she had previously considered as chaotic she now thought of as creative and empowering. After hearing a talk I gave entitled "Everything You Need to Know about Making Babies" and thinking about the truly mystical origins of children, she admitted that she was having bittersweet thoughts about her grandparents, who were Holocaust survivors, and what they had had to overcome in order to have any children at all. She had also begun to feel a sort of mystic kinship with her great-grandparents, who had been lost in the destruction of the Jews of Poland.

"Is it possible that they have been waiting for me to start exploring the deeper truths of marriage and parenting?" she asked me. "Is it possible that the decisions I am making now about having children and how I will raise my family can bring some comfort to them and their souls?"

Zoe had indeed come a long way. It seemed that something her great-grandparents had done was having a profound effect on her today and that she was tapping into their legacy. To understand how that could be and to understand the beginning of good parenting, we need to consider what takes place in the spiritual world when life begins. Life in this sense is not only about zygotes and fetuses. The real life-force of the body is in the soul, and without that vital force, there is no life. That is why God created a body and then breathed into it a living soul.[2]

At what point does the body of a baby receive its soul? That's a question that frequently arises; for whenever that takes place, we know that life has begun. In actuality, life for a baby doesn't really begin at all—it continues. The life that we give a child is a continuation of the life that was given to us. That's what Zoe was getting at as she thought about her grandparents and what they had passed on to her. It's not possible for life to start "from scratch." We can only pass on what we have been given in a continuation of that first life that God originally gave to Adam and Eve. The source deep within us that facilitates this transmission is the brain, because it's our thoughts that command the actions that follow.

What does that imply about the conception of a child? If during intimacy a husband and a wife are focused on each other and their life's mission, those thoughts are going to directly impact the child who is conceived by them. Perhaps that is why the origin of a baby is called "conception" (a word that can also refer to an idea or the result of thought), for the child's life begins with thought.

So let's rephrase our question to make it more exact: When does the fetus have a life of its own rather than being part of the life of the father and the mother? The answer is that at the moment of conception a soul is drawn down by the parents' intimacy. From that moment, the soul is connected to the physical matter that will become its body, as inconsequential as that physical matter may appear at that stage. Even though this fetus cannot really be called "a body," the soul is already present.[3] Slowly, over the nine months of pregnancy, the soul merges into the body of the baby in the womb until at birth the merger is complete.

The body is alive, then, because of the energy and vitality of the soul. The further health and well-being of the baby to be born depends on how the soul has settled within the child. If there is a disturbance or some sort of blockage preventing the soul from being completely absorbed into the body, some part of the body can fail or malfunction, resulting, for example, in illness or deformity.

Though an undeveloped body is not fully capable of sensation, the same cannot be said of a soul. The soul can see, hear, know, and feel, even when the body that hosts it cannot. As the body develops, the faculty of the soul that enables seeing is expressed in physical eyes, the faculty of the soul that enables hearing is expressed in the physical ears of the baby, and so on. That is why it is so important for a mother to be careful about what she sees, hears, and says during pregnancy—because the soul of the baby is present and fully cognizant. Stories are told of Jewish women who would sit near Torah academies while they were pregnant so that their unborn babies could benefit from the learning taking place there. Although the baby's ears were not developed, the soul of the baby was fully present and could benefit from the illuminating teachings it absorbed.

The Impact of Our Thoughts and Emotions

A child's exposure to good influences begins at the moment the mother and the father are intimate and the baby is conceived. In those moments, the parents can contribute to the sort of child that will be born out of their intimacy. The feelings of the parents, the thoughts that preoccupy them, the motives that animate them, the environment in which they choose to be together, and the mood in which they approach intimacy all have an effect on the outcome of their intimacy: the baby.

Surely every mother would agree that each baby is born with something of a personality. A baby is not a blank, not some sort of clean slate onto which the parents will write his or her personality. The baby is already born equipped with at least a nascent temperament. Some babies are born cheerful, some angry, some placid, and some irritable. We do not yet have a scientific way to explain this; certainly there is mystery here. Judaism teaches that just as it makes sense that the physical health of the parents will affect the physical health of the baby, so the parents' spiritual state at the time of conception will also affect the spirit or personality of the baby. That is why Jewish sages warn parents not to conceive a baby when they are angry or drunk or thinking of someone other than their spouses, for these states of mind and spirit will not benefit the child.[4]

For example, King David said about himself in Psalms, "I was conceived in sin."[5] The Talmud says he was referring to the fact that when he was conceived, his father, Jesse, was thinking not about David's mother but about his other wife. This story is doubly instructive. First, as King David attests, that kind of thought is detrimental. Second, although such a situation is detrimental, a child can be born from less than perfect intimacy and still rise to the greatest heights. We would all like to avoid such challenges from the outset, however, for we cannot guarantee that we will be able to rise above them as King David was able to do.

Whether or not a soul drawn down by intimacy will actually result in a baby being born is God's decision, but if it is born, the soul will be affected by the thoughts and actions of the parents. While the actual gifts and abilities of the soul are given by God, the manner in which these gifts and abilities express themselves, the so-called "garments of the soul," originate with the parents.

Although this might sound novel, it's actually not. It's a common enough perception that a child conceived from a violent rape may have the extra difficulty of anger woven into his makeup. Anger is something he must learn to deal with and overcome. If a pregnant mother is disturbed by bad news or undergoes a traumatic experience during her pregnancy, God forbid, many accept that these events could have an unpleasant effect on her unborn child. Homeopathic practitioners who treat infants will often ask about the emotional environment of a child's conception and gestation to better understand his or her health. In addition, many parents talk to their unborn children, play them music, and read poetry to them. Why? Because they believe that the baby *in utero* can be influenced in some way.

How early can this influence begin? How early can the parents' emotions begin to affect the baby's emotions? From the very moment of conception. This doesn't mean that every child who harbors some negative character trait can blame his or her parents. Just as many people get lung cancer even if they have never smoked, so a baby can be angry even if the parents were not. Nor does it mean that just because the television was on while the parents were together, distracting them from concentrating on one another, that the child will automatically have trouble concentrating. The outcome of these circumstances is not automatically negative. What we can say is that a baby's prospects improve when the parents have a healthy and respectful experience of intimacy.

The importance of bringing ourselves to our intimate encounters with conscious intention and in the right frame of mind is reflected in a story passed down about one of the famous Chassidic leaders, Rabbi Menachem Mendel of Kotzk. He once sat at a gathering of his closest disciples and made a telling statement about his relationship with his son. His disciples had been sharing stories that reflected a common theme—how well the Rebbe knew each of them—when one asked, "And your son, Rebbe, how well do you know your son?" The Kotzker replied, "I know with what thoughts I invited him into the world."

Having the right thoughts and emotions during intimacy is so important that if either partner is not in the right frame of mind, the couple should wait for a more opportune time. On the other hand, certain moments, like Shabbat evening or other devotional occasions, lend themselves to intimacy and will have a positive effect on any child conceived.

Supporting the Soul

An additional insight into what happens at spiritual levels at the moment of conception comes from another statement of King David's in which he describes the moment of conception like this: "My father and my mother have abandoned me, but the Lord will gather me in."[6] At the moment the soul of the unborn baby is brought into the womb, the parents are often asleep—they abandon the soul, so to speak. Just when the soul is looking for support, they are not there.

Why is the soul looking for support? Because at conception, the soul experiences a trauma. Why would an infinite soul want to be consigned to a limited body? So at this traumatic moment, the soul is comforted by God's presence.

The same dependence of the soul on God's protection is true at the moment of birth. In this well-known Psalm, King David is, in fact, describing the accompanying trauma of birth: "Even though I walk through the valley of the shadow of death, I will fear no evil."[7] There is a valley, a space between our life inside the womb and our life outside in the world. When the baby leaves the womb but is not yet breathing on its own, it is in the "valley" between these two worlds. The danger to the baby at this time is great, and that danger is called the "shadow of death." Again, while the baby's parents are of little help, God is there. "I fear no evil, because you are with me," says King David, acknowledging that we all as tiny infants experience and draw comfort from God's presence.

What takes place at conception—when the physical matter of a fetus is wedded to the spirit that will enliven it—as well as what takes place during gestation and birth is filled with mystery and power. It all starts with the moment of intimacy. As we have seen, all that a baby will become begins with this formative event. A husband and wife consciously participating in this moment are truly partners in creation.

*A couple's mental and emotional
state has a profound spiritual effect on the
life that will result from their union.
By being mindful at the time of conception,
parents can help give birth to a
spiritually healthy child.*

Chapter 14

....

THE AWE
OF UNION

The Awe of Union

. . . .

THE PAIN JOSH experienced when his first marriage fell apart had been so intense that he barely survived the breakup. After two years of learning how to achieve real and lasting intimacy along with many hours of honest self-reflection, Josh surprised himself. He arrived at the point where he not only thought he could succeed in a new marriage but was ready and anxious to try again. He was frankly amazed that he had come to this conclusion and even wondered if he was going a little crazy.

What *is* it that makes us want to marry? And why would we want to marry after we have failed before? Now that our society has taken away the financial penalties for remaining single, eliminated the cultural stigma of avoiding marriage, and made it okay to have the sexual privileges of marriage without being married, why would someone actually want to get married?

Maybe it's just as well that all the traditional reasons have faded away. Perhaps the only tenable and true rationale for marriage is the original one. We get married because God wants us to get married. It is part of his plan, which began with Adam and Eve and is described in Genesis: "A man shall therefore leave his father and mother and unite with his wife, and they shall become one flesh."[1]

How do we achieve that union, that oneness? As you learned earlier, Jewish sages liken the marital bedroom to the Holy of Holies—the most sacred part of the Temple, a place that belonged to God alone and was off-limits to everyone except the high priest for a brief service once a year. Even then, the high priest did not enter as a private person with personal ambitions. He could never become overly familiar with this place because it was not his. The only way he could enter the Holy of Holies was to be overwhelmed with the feeling that he didn't rightfully belong there. That feeling is called awe.

Being Invited into Your Spouse's Private Space

We often think of awe in terms of what we experience when we become aware of God's presence. Awe also applies to the most sacred space in human relationships, the connection between a husband and a wife. When a husband and wife feel awe in each other's presence, they have an overwhelming awareness of each other that causes them to momentarily forget their own selves. The suspension of focus on the self is what makes oneness possible.

If when approaching intimacy a man were to feel so at home in his wife's presence that he felt this private space was his by right, he would no longer feel any awe. The same goes for the wife. Suppose a woman was a guest in another person's home. Would she ever dare to start rearranging the furniture? Of course not. She would no longer be a guest but an intruder. The host would be justified in taking the guest to task: "Hey, who asked you to fix anything?"

We should all feel a little awe at being a guest in someone's home—and being invited into someone else's space—and never presume to alter arrangements there. Awe is a product of humility, the respectful attitude that we have no right to intrude in another's space or affairs. That is exactly how we should enter the life of our spouse. We should never become an intruder, and the way to avoid that is by recognizing that we don't ever belong in another's private space. Their private space is not ours to enter by right. Rather we are and always will be a guest, and our presence in their private space is a privilege. In a healthy marriage, two people respect each other enough never to take what isn't theirs.

When the high priest came out of the Holy of Holies, when he had succeeded in his task of the Yom Kippur offering, he celebrated with a party. It was a celebration of joy at being allowed the merit of performing this job. The awe he felt at entering the Holy of Holies was coupled with a joy at being asked to enter. In a marriage, we also experience awe at being asked to enter the intimate life of our spouse. That awe is coupled with joy and excitement—and what could be more exciting than being where we are not supposed to be but have nonetheless been invited to enter?

Never Take Intimacy for Granted

Despite the devaluation of marriage in our society, we have still retained the concept that a wife is exclusive to her husband and a husband is exclusive to his wife. Most still consider adultery dishonorable on the grounds that a husband and wife are pledged to one another. Upon closer inspection, however, there is something distasteful about the entire notion that we "save" ourselves for our spouse. What does that mean? Does a wife belong to her husband? Does a husband's private life belong to his wife? Not at all.

Indeed, the exclusive invitation to enter the space of the other is never a given. It is not issued once for all time. Likewise, a couple should never take for granted that they have achieved a permanent state of oneness or that intimacy is something they automatically and always possess. Intimacy cannot be clutched and saved like a possession. *In each physical encounter, intimacy must be achieved all over again.*

That concept dovetails with a point we covered earlier—that married couples who practice modest behavior don't talk about their intimate life. Obviously, that is not because they are trying to pretend they have no intimate life. There is a deeper reason for the modesty. A couple broadcasting what they share would sound as if they were taking their relationship for granted: "Hey, we've got this thing going on." Being quiet about intimacy doesn't mean hiding it; it means protecting it. Ultimately, it demonstrates that the couple isn't taking anything for granted.

Committed to carrying these lessons about intimacy, union, and awe into his new approach to relationships, Josh now looked forward to marriage and a shared intimacy that would impact not only his life but the life of others. That preparation held him in good stead. A few years ago I had the privilege of attending Josh's wedding. Like thousands of others, he had suffered through a life of alienation—until he learned the priceless value of intimacy. Recently, he and his wife, Jessica, became the proud parents of twin daughters. They expect that their marriage, grounded in the timeless traditions that value, respect, and cherish intimacy and family, will prove a rich foundation for their children to fashion their own intimate lives when the time comes for them to do so.

Marriage is still as important as it ever was. Physical and spiritual union with another person has always been the most exalted of any human experience. It is a unique and joyful departure from the often lonely experience of living our lives as separate beings. Intimacy is at the heart—the ecstatic heart—of what it means to be married. We must approach every moment of intimacy with awe, for we enter sacred territory. We must remove our shoes, for it is holy ground.

*The awe we feel at being invited
into the private space of our spouse is
the most important element of intimacy.
Enveloped in that awe we forget
ourselves, making the experience
of oneness possible.*

Epilogue

....

THE TRANSFORMATIVE POWER OF TRUE INTIMACY

The Transformative Power
of True Intimacy

. . . .

FOR ALL OF US, intimacy is an essential need. We long for intimacy because without it we feel incomplete. You will have many opportunities in your life—opportunities to do good deeds, to grow and learn, to make a difference in other people's lives and in your community. But probably at no other time in your life will you have the opportunity to experience the wholeness that you feel in moments of true intimacy.

Intimacy, as we've seen, is not about focusing on ourselves—and it's more than just a physical connection. Intimacy is physical, emotional, *and* soulful. It embraces and then goes beyond the physical to the highest pleasure, the pleasure of oneness that only true intimacy can bring. In the moment of intimacy, we enter the innocent place in our soul that leaves us feeling more in touch with our essence than before. Through that experience of oneness, we also have the opportunity to dissolve into something cosmic, something bigger than the sum of our parts.

Through these pages, you have explored some of the deeper truths at the heart of our longing for intimacy. You've also read about the obstacles to intimacy that are at the root of society's serious intimacy crisis. In addition, you've gained insights and strategies, taken from Jewish tradition and the little-known but valuable mystical traditions of Kabbalah, that provide the key to overcoming those obstacles and cultivating a healthy and fulfilling intimate life.

You've learned about creating a sacred space where husband and wife can enjoy their deepest knowledge of one another, where all distractions to intimacy are eliminated. You've seen how periodically creating a "divide," by drawing apart and coming together again, keeps the spark of intimacy alive. And you've discovered how essential it is to cultivate a sense of respect and awe at the privilege of being invited once again into your spouse's life and private space.

You've also learned about the dynamics of giving and receiving and come to understand that the act of intimacy is empowered by our awareness of its spiritual force and potential for life. In addition, you now know that intimacy is something that must be practiced and nurtured—and that it's up to each of us to create the conditions for intimacy to flourish.

Most importantly, and underlying all of this, the sages tell us that through intimacy you have the opportunity to affect your own personal life as well as the lives of many others in a positive way. No matter where people have lived or in what century, they have always desired to lead lives of significance. It is part of being human to want to somehow contribute to making the world more enlightened, peaceful, civil, and moral. On the other hand, it's easy to feel frustrated, not knowing where to begin or exactly how to pitch in. What can one person do to make a difference?

In truth, all change begins with one person. That's not an empty platitude; it's plain fact. Morally strong and healthy societies are composed of morally strong and healthy families, and at the heart of a moral, healthy family is a moral, healthy couple. Just two individuals.

It may seem incredible that the way two people choose to behave with one another in complete privacy can actually affect the whole world, but that is the truth. All we have to do is look at what happens when the opposite is the case. The results of abandoning modesty, respect, and sanctity in personal relationships are real and they are painful, measured in emotional distress, marital breakdown, and children who grow up in broken homes.

Simply put, intimacy can be powerfully transformative. By transforming our own attitudes about love, intimacy, and sexuality and putting into practice the keys that have been passed on to us, not only will we bring about fulfilling and lasting relationships, but together we'll be setting the world aright—one bedroom at a time.

ACKNOWLEDGMENTS

WITH GOD'S BLESSING and kindness this book has come to fruition, and I am deeply grateful to him for the opportunity to be engaged in such a meaningful endeavor. To bring a book like this across the finish line requires the contributions of many people, and I would like to take this opportunity to thank those who have been so helpful in its preparation.

First and foremost, my thanks go to Ricardo Adler for inviting me to partner with him in the making and production of the documentary film *The Lost Key*. His vision for both the film and the book was inspiring and his enthusiasm unflagging.

I would also like to thank Chana Greenberg for all of her hard work in drawing from the resources in the thousands of hours of my recorded lectures to compile the first drafts of this book and make it a reality; Fernanda Rossi for her helpful suggestions on the text; Susanna Margolis and Uriela Sagiv for their fine editorial work and expert advice. Thanks also to Nigel J. Yorwerth and Patricia Spadaro for their excellent publishing coaching, guidance, editing, and shepherding of this book to completion as well as enthusiastically representing this book for foreign and translation rights throughout the world.

My gratitude also goes to the following families for their support: the Cohen, Friedman, Trestman, New, Morrow, Wexler, and Levin families.

A special thank you goes to my son Rabbi Zalman Friedman for his devoted supervision of the entire project.

And most importantly, I am grateful for the support of my wife, Chana, and our sons and daughters, who encouraged me in this.

NOTES

Chapter 1

1. Esther Perel, *Mating in Captivity,* http://www.powells .com/essays/perel.html.

Chapter 2

1. Genesis 1:27.

2. Talmud, *Sotah*, 2b.

Chapter 4

1. Maimonides, *Sefer HaMitzvot*, Mitzvah #353 (based on Leviticus 18:6).

2. Talmud, *Kiddushin* 80b (based on Deuteronomy 13:7).

Chapter 5

1. *Shulchan Aruch* (Code of Jewish Law), Orach Chayim 240:7.

Chapter 6

1. Genesis 3:16.
2. Genesis 3:20.

Chapter 7

1. Genesis 4:1.

Chapter 8

1. The sages liken marital intimacy to peace in the home (*Shabbos* 152) and remark that this type of peace is "great" (*Chulin* 141a). Increasing the level of intimacy, love, and desire between husband and wife also positively affects the children they will bear together (*Sefer Chassidim* 362).

Chapter 9

1. Maimonides, *Sefer Hashorashim*, Shoresh #11.
2. Maimonides, *Mishneh Torah*, Hilchos Deos, Chapter 5, Halacha 8.
3. Talmud, *Nedarim* 20b, and *Shulchan Aruch* (Code of Jewish Law), Orach Chayim 140:3; see also Nachmanides' *Igeret HaKodesh.*
4. Nachmanides, *Igeret HaKodesh* (Chapter 5): "They should be thinking about the mitzvah they are doing, the possibility of creating holy souls, and that their attachment connects to holy sources and draws down the holy upper light."

Chapter 10

1. Talmud, *Megillah* 29a, where it states that God will dwell in the holy spaces we create, for they are the Temple in miniature.

2. Talmud, *Niddah* 31a.

3. Talmud, *Eruvin* 100b.

4. Talmud, *Sotah* 17a.

5. Talmud, *Nedarim* 20b.

Chapter 11

1. Cole Porter, "Let's Do It, Let's Fall in Love" from the musical *Paris* (1928).

2. Talmud, *Shabbat* 86a, *Ketubot* 65b, and *Niddah* 17a.

3. Talmud, *Ketubot* 48a; *Shulchan Aruch* (Code of Jewish Law), Even HaEzer 76:13; Rashi on *Shabbat* 13a (based on Genesis 2:24).

4. *Shulchan Aruch* (Code of Jewish Law), Orach Chayim 240:5.

5. *Shulchan Aruch* (Code of Jewish Law), Orach Chayim 240:4; Rama, Even HaEzer 25:2.

6. Talmud, *Pesachim* 72b, *Ketubot* 63a, and *Nedarim* 15b and 81b (based on Exodus 21:10).

7. *Mishnah Berurah* 240:2.

8. See Rabbi Yitzchak Luria (Arizal), *Taamei Hamitzvos* and Rabbi Chaim Dovid Azulay (the Chidah) *Midbar Kdaimot*, p. 83.

Chapter 12

1. *Shulchan Aruch* (Code of Jewish Law), Yoreh Deah, Hilchot Niddah (based on Leviticus 18:19).

Chapter 13

1. Furstenberg, F.F., Nord, C.W., Peterson, J.L., and Zill, N. (1983). "The Life Course of Children of Divorce." *American Sociological Review* 48 (5), pp. 656–68.

2. Genesis 2:7.

3. See *Likutei Sichos* vol. 2, p. 602.

4. Talmud, *Nedarim* 20b.

5. Psalms 51:7.

6. Psalms 27:10.

7. Psalms 23:4.

Chapter 14

1. Genesis 2:24.

Learn more about
Rabbi Manis Friedman and his work

Rabbi Manis Friedman regularly speaks and teaches at events worldwide. He offers free online tips and resources as well as ongoing releases on a wide range of topics, including relationships, dating, marriage and family, emotional well-being, spirituality, life's challenges, and much more.

Sign up for Rabbi Friedman's free email newsletter to get exclusive content, updates, and special offers at:

www.itsgoodtoknow.org

Stay connected:

facebook.com/manisfriedman
youtube.com/manisfriedman
twitter.com/manisfriedman

thejoyofintimacy.com
itsgoodtoknow.org
info@itsgoodtoknow.org

RABBI MANIS FRIEDMAN is a world-renowned author, counselor, teacher, and speaker, well known for his provocative and incisive wit and wisdom. His international speaking tours, seminars, and retreats take him around the world, and he has been featured on CNN, A&E Reviews, PBS, and BBC Worldwide as well as in such publications as *The New York Times, Rolling Stone, Seventeen, Guideposts,* and *Publishers Weekly*. His first book, *Doesn't Anyone Blush Anymore?* (published by Harper San Francisco), was widely praised by the media. He has hosted his own critically acclaimed cable television series syndicated throughout North America.

Rabbi Friedman is featured in the award-winning documentary *The Lost Key*. He is the dean of Bais Chana Institute of Jewish Studies, which he cofounded in 1971, and the founder of It's Good to Know, a nonprofit life-learning foundation based in New York City. He lives with his family in St. Paul, Minnesota. To learn more about Rabbi Manis Friedman and his work, visit ItsGoodToKnow.org.

Ricardo Adler is an award-winning filmmaker whose passion is to transform audiences through the beauty of Jewish wisdom. His latest release is *The Lost Key: Rediscover Intimacy*, a joint effort with Rabbi Manis Friedman. The film had a successful festival run worldwide, won an award for best documentary, received positive reviews from film critics, and was featured in *The Daily Beast, Los Angeles Times, CNN en Español, America TeVe/Fox Mundo, The Jewish Journal,* and other publications. For more information, visit thelostkey.com.

Previously, Ricardo Adler released two documentaries that met with success in more than 20 countries, including *Mazal Tov: What You Didn't Know About Jewish Marriage*, which has generated 100,000+ downloads. Before becoming a filmmaker, he earned a degree in engineering at Stanford followed by a successful career in high-tech serving Fortune 500 companies. He has been featured in major publications such as *Machine Design, Artificial Intelligence in Engineering,* and *MacWorld.* Ricardo lives in Venezuela with his family.